DEMONS AND DELIVERANCE

IN THE MINISTRY OF JESUS

by

Frank D. Hammond

Demons and Deliverance in the Ministry of Jesus,
by Frank Hammond
ISBN #0-89228-001-8
Copyright ©, 1991

Impact Christian Books, Inc.
332 Leffingwell Ave., Suite 101,
Kirkwood, MO 63122
314-822-3309

February, 1991 First Printing
August, 1984 Second Printing
April, 1998 Third Printing
January, 2001 Fourth Printing
February, 2003, Fifth Printing

Printed in the United States of America

The *American Revised Edition* (1901) of the Bible is used throughout, unless otherwise indicated.

PREFACE

After twenty years of intense involvement in deliverance ministry, I came to a crossroads. For all those years I had been active as pastor of a local church, and kept in doctrinal balance by the need to preach the whole counsel of God to a local assembly. Now, I faced the call of God to a full-time work in spiritual warfare. The call to a traveling ministry would necessitate my resignation from the local pastorate, and meant that I would be specializing in deliverance teaching. I sensed a specific danger involved in specializing in one field: the danger of doctrinal imbalance.

I had seen others fall into imbalance, but the error of others was not an excuse for me to refuse God's call. I had, in fact, already faced the temptation of going down doctrinal "rabbit trails" as an escape from repetitive teaching. While in prayer about this concern for imbalance, the Holy Spirit said to my heart, "Stick with the meat and potatoes of deliverance." I understood this meant that I was to stick with basic principles of deliverance and to keep the teaching and the ministry based on scripture.

The most helpful principles of deliverance are those found in the teachings and activities of Jesus Himself. This is why I have undertaken to write this study from the Synoptic Gospels. This book is set forth with the prayer that it will help others, both on the giving and receiving ends of deliverance ministry, to maintain integrity and avoid pitfalls by adhering to basic scriptural principles.

1991

ACKNOWLEDGMENTS

The task of writing increases in ease and enjoyment when there are those who stand beside the writer to encourage, advise and assist. I have been especially blessed in all these ways.

First, I joyously thank Ida Mae, my wife and companion in ministry. Together we have learned through study and experience the principles of deliverance set forth, and together we have put these deliverance truths into writing.

My special thanks to our partners in ministry, through whose prayers we have been spiritually strengthened and through whose love gifts we have been physically supported. With their help, Ida Mae and I have been able to take several months sabbatical and finish the manuscript.

I offer special appreciation to Sydna Loden, a faithful friend, who with joy, enthusiasm and literary skill has set her mark on most of the pages of this manuscript.

Frank Hammond
Plainview, Texas

CONTENTS

Preface   iii
Introduction   1

TOPICS:

The Wilderness Temptations   3
The Gospel Of The Kingdom   11
Deliverance: A Public Ministry   13
Deliverance In The Atonement   33
Ministering To The Multitude   37
Continued Ministry To The Multitude   41
Prayer For Deliverance   43
The Test Of True Discipleship   45
The Testimony Of Miracles   49
Healed Of Demons   53
Two Opposing Kingdoms   57
Filling The House   63
Parable Of The Sower   79
Parable of The Tares   81
The Gadarene Demoniac   83
Another Deliverance Healing And Blasphemous
    Accusation   87
The Twelve Commissioned And Anointed   89
Persecution Encountered   95
Deliverance Is The Children's Bread   99
Binding And Loosing   103
Men Used Of God Are Sometimes Used Of Satan   107
A Deliverance Failure   109
Exclusiveness Rebuked   115
Enforcing Church Discipline   117
The Curse of Unforgiveness   119

The Mission Of The Seventy   121
The Spirit of Infirmity   125
Attempted Intimidation   129
Satan Enters Into Judas   131
Satan Asks For Peter   135

INTRODUCTION

Jesus encountered the devil in the wilderness temptations at the very outset of His public ministry. Immediately thereafter, He began to cast demons out of multitudes of people. As soon as He had chosen the twelve, He began to teach them to cast out demons; He then sent them out with the commission and anointing to do so. Thus, the synoptic gospels give tremendous insight into the existence and activities of Satan and his demon spirits. Also, believers are taught how to overcome evil spirits with confidence.

There are many activities of the devil recorded throughout these gospels which are not expressly attributed to him. For example, the devil determined from the birth of Jesus that he would somehow destroy the Christchild. Satan, the murderer, worked through King Herod to kill the child, Jesus, by a wholesale murder of male children. After the ministry of Jesus was begun, Satan worked principally through the Jewish religious leaders who made plots and took steps to kill Him; but all of the devil's attempts, whether direct or indirect, were unsuccessful. Jesus was destined to die on the cross for man's sins, and Satan could not kill him prematurely.

Furthermore, the devil was at work in all the events leading up to and including the crucifixion. When the blood of Jesus was poured out, the devil assumed he had won; but, the very thing he thought of as victory became the instrument of his own defeat:

> We speak wisdom, however, among them that are full grown: yet a wisdom not of this world, nor of the rulers of

1

this world, who are coming to nought: but we speak God's wisdom in a mystery, even the wisdom that hath been hidden, which God foreordained before the worlds unto our glory: which none of the rulers of this world hath known: for had they known it, they would not have crucified the Lord of glory. I Corinthians 2:6-8

In the study of the synoptics it should, therefore, be noted that many activities of Satan are not specifically identified as such. In this particular study we have extracted only the direct references to Satanic activity. The accounts are taken in chronological order, following Dr. A.T. Robertson's, *The Harmony Of The Gospels.* Where accounts are found in more than one Gospel, all the references are given, and the reference to the Gospel quoted is highlighted in bold print.

THE WILDERNESS TEMPTATIONS

Mark 1:12-13; **Matthew 4:1-11;** Luke 4:1-13

1 Then was Jesus led up of the Spirit into the
2 wilderness to be tempted of the devil. And
   when he had fasted forty days and forty
3 nights, he afterward hungered. And the
   tempter came and said unto him, If thou art
   the Son of God, command that these stones
4 become bread. But he answered and said, It
   is written, Man shall not live by bread alone,
   but by every word that proceedeth out of the
5 mouth of God. Then the devil taketh him into
   the holy city; and he set him on the pinnacle
6 of the temple, and saith unto him, If thou art
   the Son of God, cast thyself down: for it is
   written,

>   He shall give his angels charge
>   concerning thee:
>   And on their hands they shall
>   bear thee up,
>   Lest haply thou dash thy foot
>   against a stone.

7 Jesus said unto him, Again it is written, Thou
   shall not make trial of the Lord thy God.
8 Again the devil taketh him unto an exceeding
   high mountain, and sheweth him all the

3

kingdoms of the world, and the glory of them;

9 and he said unto him, All these things will I give thee, if thou wilt fall down and worship

10 me. Then saith Jesus unto him, Get thee hence, Satan: for it is written, Thou shalt worship the Lord thy God, and him only shalt

11 thou serve. Then the devil leaveth him; and behold angels came and ministered unto him.

Led Of The Spirit

Jesus had just been baptized by John, and as He came up out of the waters of the Jordan River, "lo, the heavens were opened unto him (John), and he saw the Spirit of God descending like a dove, and coming upon him (Jesus)" (Matthew 3:16). Thus, Jesus was anointed of the Holy Spirit for the ministry for which He had been sent.[1] "Then" (immediately) Jesus was led up of the Spirit into the wilderness for a confrontation with the devil.

Why would the Holy Spirit purposely lead Jesus into a direct confrontation with the devil? He did so because Jesus had come into the world for this very confrontation: "To this end was the Son of God manifested, that he might destroy the works of the devil" (I John 3:8).

Undoubtedly, few Christians have considered that it is God's plan that they also be in direct confrontation with the devil.

> Yet, just as surely as the Holy Spirit led Jesus into such an encounter, the believer will also be led to face the devil, for the believer is commissioned to do so.[2]

An example is found in my own life of the Holy Spirit's leading an anointed believer into confrontation with the devil. Twenty four hours following my anointing for ministery through the baptism in the Holy Spirit, I was thrust

---

1 Acts 10:37-38.
2 Mark 16:17.

into confrontation with demon spirits. I had just given a testimony of my baptism in the Holy Spirit at a Full Gospel Businessmen's convention. Before I left the platform, three disheveled hippies came uninvitedly to the platform and interrupted the meeting. Even as I saw them coming toward the podium, to my amazement I exclaimed to the pastor sitting next to me, "Those men are not in the spirit of the Lord." Then, pointing at the hippie leading the way, I declared, "That man has a demon!" The leading hippie, who was disheveled and whose eyes were glazed by drugs, then took the microphone and declared, "I am Jesus. I am the way!" At this precise moment my wife, Ida Mae, also under the Holy Spirit's leading, from the back of the auditorium pointed her finger toward the platform and shouted, "I rebuke you, demon, in the name of Jesus!" Whereupon, all three hippies fell like sacks of potatoes to the platform, smitten by the power God.

Neither my wife nor I had ever before recognized or challenged demonic activity in a person, yet what the Holy Spirit did through each of us was absolutely scriptural. The two of us had just been anointed through the baptism in the Holy Spirit for empowered ministry. As with Jesus, we were immediately thrust into confrontation with the devil.

Jesus has declared that His Church will be a militant church, taking the offensive against Satan's powers: "Upon this rock I will build my church; and the gates of Hades shall not prevail against it" (Matthew 16:18). Every believer in Jesus Christ is identified with His Church and is called to attack "the gates of Hades".

Spiritual warfare is every Christian's calling.

The Devil As Tempter

In his attacks against Jesus, the devil took the role of tempter. Temptation is one of his three main tactics. Every attack that the devil makes against mankind is either through the channel of temptation, accusation or deception.

Jesus prepared Himself through fasting for this confrontation with the devil. Thus,

> Jesus makes plain to us that fasting is important to spiritual warfare.

In fact, fasting is a spiritual discipline which every Christian is expected to practice. Jesus did not say "if" you fast; He said "when" you fast (see: Matthew 6:16). On one occasion when the disciples were unable to cast out a certain demon, Jesus explained that "this kind goeth not out save by prayer and fasting" (Matthew 17:21, Margin).

The devil is also an opportunist. He knew that Jesus was hungry at the end of forty days of fasting. Any fast longer than forty days would of necessity be supernatural, for after that length of time the body has used up its reserve energy stored in the fat, and starvation sets in. So the devil's first temptation was that Jesus, independent of the Father's will, supply food for Himself by turning stones into bread.

There is a parallel between the devil's temptation of Jesus and that of Eve in the garden of Eden. In both temptations the devil appealed to the lust of the flesh, and in both temptations the devil threw doubt upon the Word of God. He said to Eve, "Hath God said?," and to Jesus he challenged, "If thou art the Son of God..."

God had spoken clearly to Eve that she was not to eat of the tree of the knowledge of good and evil. The devil challenged the validity of God's word so as to rob her of the authority by which temptation is to be resisted.

As for Jesus, the devil attempted the same tactic: "If thou art the son of God" (Matthew 4:3). Now, Jesus had just come from the baptismal waters of Jordan where the voice of the Father declared from heaven, "This is my beloved Son, in whom I am well pleased" (Matthew 3:17). So by the testimony of the Father, Jesus is the Son of God.

Jesus was not moved by the devil's attempt to discredit God's Word. As always, Satan seeks to cast doubt upon the Word of God. He fears the light and power inherent in the Word.

The Tempter is defeated by using the "sword of the Spirit, which is the word of God" (Ephesians 6:17). Eve should have told the serpent that God had expressly said that she was not to eat of the fruit of the tree of the knowledge of good and evil, and that she was standing on that word. In such a way, she would have resisted the devil and caused him to flee.[3]

Jesus overcame the devil's temptation to yield to the appetite of the flesh by responding, "It is written, Man shall not live by bread alone, but by every word that proceedeth out of the mouth of God" (Matthew 4:4). Thus Jesus thrust Satan with the sword of the Spirit with a quotation from Deuteronomy 8:3.

> The Word of God is a powerful weapon, and we must never let it slip or become dull.

The devil will try in every way that he can to convince the Christian warrior to substitute something else in place of the Word. Psychology and worldly counsel will not phase the devil. Stand on the Word of God. Joshua was instructed by God on how to guarantee success in warfare: Do not let the Word of God depart out of your mouth, meditate upon it day and night and do what God's Word says (see: Joshua 1:8).

In the second temptation the devil appealed to the pride of life. He offered promotion of self. He approached Eve with the lie that if she and Adam would only eat the forbidden fruit, they would "be as God" (Genesis 3:5). The devil continues to spread his "be as God" lie through "New Age" advocates who swallow the Hindu error that men become gods through the repeated karmas of reincarna-

---

3 James 4:7.

7

tion. Mormons also propagate the falsehood that men become gods. Let us beware of all false teachers who appeal to human pride through this lie of the devil.

Pride is called "the condemnation of the devil" (I Timothy 3:6). That is, pride is the same condemnation into which the devil fell.[4] The devil is full of pride, and he wants all men to come under that same condemnation.

In the identical appeal to pride, the devil tempted Jesus to jump from the pinnacle and let the angels rescue Him. The devil was offering Jesus a spectacular way to gain recognition and acceptance outside the will of God.

It should be noted that when Jesus put down the first temptation with a quotation from Scripture, it was as though the devil said, "Oh, so you intend to stand on Scripture, do you? Well, let me tell you what the Word says." Satan uses Scripture against those who stand on the Word. For example, he tempts those who respect the Word to follow the letter of the law rather than the spirit of the law, for he knows very well that the letter of the law killeth and the spirit giveth life. Thus, one may stand upon the Word in a blind legalism that leads to foolish interpretations of scripture or to a bibliolatry that excessively venerates the written word above a personal relationship with God.

The third temptation was directed toward the lust of the eye. In Eve's case the Tempter showed her that the tree was "a delight to the eyes" (Genesis 3:6). In like temptation he showed Jesus the kingdoms of this world and their glory. Thus, he tempted both Eve and Jesus to accept the glamour of the world as a substitute for the will of God. By the way in which Jesus resisted this temptation, He demonstrated to us that we cannot bargain with the devil. The price tag is too high. Satan demands that men worship him. The would-be usurper of God's throne lusts for the worship due only unto God. To have man's worship is Satan's highest aspiration.

Jesus said, "Get thee hence." Thus, Satan was commanded to flee. He would get no recognition from Jesus,

---

4 Isaiah 14:12-14.

much less worship. Let it be understood that anyone who worships Satan is immediately captured by him. One becomes his slave and is brought into the severest of bondages. On the other hand, to worship and serve God results in freedom and life.

When we submit to God and resist the devil, the devil will flee from us.[5] To submit to God is to do God's will.

> By doing what God tells us to do we become qualified to tell the devil what he must do.

God gives His authority to His own. All believers have the name of Jesus as a power of attorney; they can act in the authority of that Name and can get the same results that Jesus enjoyed during His earthly ministry.

The sword of the Spirit is wielded through speech. We must open our mouths and speak the Word of God with God-given authority.

Satan will wear us down if we allow him to hang around. We must not ignore him but rather be aggressive to resist him and drive him away.

The Ministry Of Angels

There are angels and demons everywhere. Each believer has at least one angel following him wherever he goes. When Peter knocked at the door after being supernaturally released from prison, his friends thought it was "his angel" at the door.[6]

> When the believer walks in the Spirit doing the will of God, the angels are able to assist the believer and minister to him.

---

5 James 4:7.
6 Acts 12:15.

On the other hand, if the believer is disobedient and walks in rebellion to the will of God, he opens himself to demonic influence, interference, and potential invasion. We continually choose our master by the decisions we make:

> Know ye not, that to whom ye present yourselves as servants unto obedience, his servants ye are to whom ye obey; whether of sin unto death, or of obedience unto righteousness?
>
> Romans 6:16

Notice that in the above Scripture the master is a "whom", a person, rather than an impersonal influence.

If one is not serving the Lord, he is serving the devil. There is no neutral ground.

THE GOSPEL OF THE KINGDOM

Matthew 4:23-25; Mark 1:39

23 And Jesus went about in all Galilee, teaching in their synagogues, and preaching the gospel of the kingdom, and healing all manner of disease and all manner of sickness among the

24 people. And the report of him went forth into all Syria: and they brought unto him all that were sick, holden with divers diseases and torments, possessed with devils, and epileptic, and palsied; and he healed them.

25 And there followed him great multitudes from Galilee and Decapolis and Jerusalem and Judaea and from beyond Jordan.

Through Jesus the Gospel of the Kingdom was proclaimed and manifested. His Gospel includes healing and deliverance. Those who were demonized were healed through deliverance. The Greek word for "healed" in verse twenty-four is *therapeuo,* which literally means the care and attendance necessary to bring one back to wholeness. *Therapeuo* strongly suggests a process of deliverance.

The Gospel is the good news that Jesus, the Saviour (the Deliverer), has come to bring deliverance and healing to the whole man. The spirit of man is delivered from death by the quickening power of the Holy Spirit, and the body and personality made whole through His healing touch and/or by deliverance from unclean spirits.

11

The multitudes are needy and desperate today just as they were in the days of Jesus. The Gospel has not changed nor lost its power. Jesus has not changed! He is the same yesterday, today and forever.

> Healing and deliverance remain for us as provisions of Christ's atoning work.

Healing and deliverance are companion ministries, for there are often overlapping needs. The epileptic may have a demon, but he may also need a healing of brain tissue. Whatever the need, we must learn to come to Jesus in faith, knowing that He is the Savior, Deliverer and Great Physician.

DELIVERANCE —
A PUBLIC MINISTRY

Mark 1:21-28; Luke 4:31-37

21 And they go into Capernaum; and straightway on the sabbath day he entered into the

22 synagogue and taught. And they were astonished at his teaching: for he taught them as

23 having authority, and not as the scribes. And
straightway there was in their synagogue a
man with an unclean spirit; and he cried

24 out, saying, What have we to do with thee,
Jesus thou Nazarene? art thou come to
destroy us? I know thee who thou art, the

25 Holy One of God. And Jesus rebuked him,
saying, Hold thy peace, and come out of him.

26 And the unclean spirit, tearing him and cry-

27 ing with a loud voice, came out of him. And
they were all amazed, insomuch that they
questioned among themselves, saying, What
is this? a new teaching! with authority he
commandeth even the unclean spirits, and

28 they obey him. And the report of him went
out straightway everywhere into all the region
of Galilee round about.

Anointed Teaching Excites Demons

Jesus entered the synagogue on the sabbath and began to teach. The casting out of the demon may have been more spectacular than the teaching; nevertheless, teaching was a priority with Jesus.

> Teaching is a necessary balance to the ministry of deliverance, and is often the prelude to deliverance.

Sound Bible teaching exposes the enemy; it is light brought against the kingdom of darkness.

The people were astonished at the doctrine of Jesus. We assume that His teaching that day was on deliverance, although it is not specifically stated. At least it was on a subject that excited the demons in the man who was demonized.

The first thing that impressed the worshippers in the synagogue was the authority with which Jesus taught, a contrast to the regular teachers in the synagogue. Jesus' teaching stirred up demons to a demonstrative pitch, while that of other teachers posed no threat to them. Likewise, demons are not threatened by the teaching and preaching that goes on in some churches today. A watered down, social gospel may not offend men, but neither does it offend demons! However, strong, authoritative teaching spoken in faith causes every demon present to tremble.

I am reminded of a time when I preached a sermon on "Power in the Blood". Suddenly a woman began to scream, or rather, a demon in the woman cried out, just as recorded in Mark 1:23. While the congregation sang softly, the demons were cast out of her. Then, her husband began to scream, and he, too, received deliverance. We learned that this couple had come to the service reluctantly at the insistence of a relative. They came in a mocking attitude, but the message on the blood of Jesus excited the demons in them, leading to the outburst.

A Worshipper In Need

The man with the unclean spirit must have been a regular worshipper. There is no reason to assume that he was some heathen outsider who wandered into the synagogue. He could well have been one of the leaders of the synagogue. In the same way, it is very common for persons today who truly love the Lord and worship Him with all their hearts to be troubled by evil spirits.

> One does not need to go outside the church to find those in need of deliverance.

Can Christians Be Demon Possessed?

No, a redeemed child of God cannot be owned by the devil! To *redeem* means "to release by paying a ransom price". The price paid by Jesus for our redemption was His own blood:

> Knowing that ye were redeemed, not with corruptible things, with silver or gold... but with precious blood, as of a lamb without blemish and without spot, even the blood of Christ.
>
> I Peter 1:18,19

Therefore, a Christian is His purchased possession, "for ye were bought with a price" (I Corinthians 6:20).

> A Christian is Jesus possessed, not demon possessed.

Much misunderstanding has resulted from the King James version having translated the Greek word *daimonizomai* as "possessed with devils". A more accurate translation of *daimonizomai* is: "to be under the power of a demon."[7] There is a vast difference between being pos-

---

7 Thayer's *Greek-English Lexicon.*

15

sessed (owned) by demons and by having demons. Webster renders *possessed* in reference to demons as, "affected by demons or invisible agents".[8]

The proper question is not "Can a Christian be demon possessed?" but rather, "Can a Christian have a demon or be under the power of demons"?

> An honest assessment of New Testament teaching must bring us to the conclusion that the New Testament makes no distinction between believers and non-believers as far as demonization is concerned.

Therefore, if the New Testament makes no such distinction, then none should be made. The obvious conclusion is that both unbelievers and believers can be demonized.

How can we understand the demonization of a Christian? The question faced is: Can property owned by one person be trespassed upon by another person? Suppose a landowner has a wooded piece of property that affords good squirrel hunting. A trespasser can come upon that property and begin to shoot squirrels, but he can also be put off the property as one who has no legal right. This is precisely what takes place when a demon indwells a Christian. The evil spirit has no rights of ownership. Therefore, when the evil spirit is commanded to go, by the Owner or His delegated authority, the evil spirit has no choice but to go. Trespassers can be evicted.

> Deliverance for Christians represents the eviction of trespassing spirits.

---

8 *American Dictionary of the English Language.* Noah Webster, 1828.

Another pertinent question is: "For whom is deliverance provided?" Jesus called deliverance "the children's bread" (Matthew 15:26), meaning that deliverance from demons is for those who have faith in Christ Jesus. Jesus declared that the children's bread was not to be given to "dogs", meaning those who are ceremonially impure, or those outside the covenant of God. The gentile woman of Canaan, who was seeking deliverance for her little daughter, exhibited faith by her contention that even dogs are allowed the crumbs that fall from the master's table. Whereon, Jesus declared, "O woman, great is thy faith: be it unto thee even as thou wilt. And her daughter was healed from that hour" (Matthew 15:28).

When evil spirits are driven out of a person, a spiritual condition is created which Jesus compared to a newly vacated house. He taught that if the "house" (person's life) is left unoccupied, it is susceptible to the return of the old tenant and his friends. Only a believer can fill his life with the things of Christ.

One who does not fill himself with Jesus and an opposite lifestyle from which he was delivered, is in imminent danger of ending up seven times worse than he was before.[9]

Demon Manifestations

Referring again to the man in Capernaum, when Mark 1:23 records, "and he cried out," the Scripture is referring to the demon rather than the man, although the demon used the voice of the man. Any experienced deliverance minister can tell you that evil spirits often cry out through those needing or receiving deliverance, especially when the demons are exposed to an atmosphere charged with the power of the Holy Spirit.

---

9 Matthew 12:43-45.

> It is common for demons to reveal their presence by overpowering the one indwelled.

Too, anointed preaching and teaching flush unclean spirits out of hiding. Demons are well aware of the danger they face when persons are present who can discern them and who have faith to cast them out. Demons will react out of fear and betray their presence as did this one.

An alert minister leading a church service will take note of disturbances causing distraction and confusion in the meeting. Demons may cause babies to cry or excite religious exhibitionism in adults. Anything that is not of the Holy Spirit must be dealt with, whether it be flesh or demon.

Plurality of Demons

The demon which spoke through the man in Capernaum was not alone, for there were other indwelling spirits. The pronouns in this passage alternate from the singular to the plural. For example, "He (singular) cried out, saying, what have we (plural) to do with thee...art thou come to destroy us (plural)? I (singular) know thee..." (Mark 1:23,24). The spokesman demon was the strong man, or ruler spirit. He was in charge of the demonic operation within this man. As in the case of Legion (Luke 8:26-40), we find that a demonized person may be indwelled with a rank of spirits. They are set up as a coordinated system of evil with the lesser spirits under the authority of a leader.

> An array of demons, rather than an assortment of unrelated spirits, is the challenge encountered in each deliverance situation.

One never faces "a" demon except in the sense of a

"strong man."[10] Each demon has direct connections with the demonic kingdom.

Insights Gained

Note the following insights concerning demons which are reflected in what this unclean spirit said:

1. Demons want nothing to do with Jesus. They have nothing in common with Him. They do not want an open confrontation with either Jesus or, we may add, with His disciples who bear His authority.

2. Demons know who Jesus is. At that point in time the demon in the man in Capernaum knew the identity of Jesus as the "Holy One of God." However, very few men of the time even suspected who He was. Likewise, demons also know and recognize the anointed servants of the Lord. On another occasion we read, "And the evil spirit answered and said unto them (the sons of Sceva), Jesus I know, and Paul I know; but who are ye?" (Acts 19:15).

3. Demons know they are destined for destruction and are fearful of it. [Compare: "And behold, they (demons) cried out, saying, What have we to do with thee, thou Son of God? art thou come hither to torment us before the time" (Matthew 8:29).]

Demon-Speaking Silenced

Jesus rebuked the spirit for speaking. Demons can be permitted to speak or kept from speaking by those who have authority over them. Jesus stopped the spirit from speaking, for there was nothing positive to be gained by it.

> The objective in deliverance is not to get a demon to speak but to cast it out.

---

10 Matthew 12:29; Mark 3:27; Luke 11:21.

Reasons Why We Should Not Converse With Demons.

1. We should follow the example of Jesus. When Jesus was teaching in the synagogue one day, a man with an evil spirit cried out. Jesus recognized that it was an evil spirit crying out through the man. "And Jesus rebuked him, saying, Hold thy peace, and come out of him" (Mark 1:25). The evil spirit was willing to speak, but Jesus did not use the occasion as an opportunity to converse with the demon nor to interrogate him. Again Scripture reinforces, "He also drove out many demons, but he would not let the demons speak because they knew who he was" (Mark 1:34 NIV).

Demons are anti-Christ in all that they say and do. Therefore, what they say is never a valid witness to the Person of Christ. We should never accept their testimony as a basis for validating any truth. Even when what they say is true, as in Mark 1:24, the testimony is unacceptable. God will not use the witness of demons to herald His Gospel.

For example, a demon of divination in a girl testified that Paul and Silas were, "servants of the Most High God, who proclaim unto you the way of salvation" (Acts 16:17). Instead of being pleased over the flattering words spoken by the demon, these men of God were "grieved" (KJ), and "troubled" (NIV) and "sorely annoyed" (Amplified). Finally, Paul became so troubled that he turned around and said to the spirit, "I charge thee in the name of Jesus Christ to come out of her" (Acts 16:18).

2. Evil spirits are all liars and deceivers. They have the same nature as the "father of lies." the devil. Jesus said, "He (Satan) was a murderer from the beginning, not holding to the truth, for there is no truth in him. When he lies, he speaks his native language, for he is a liar and the father of lies" (John 8:44 NIV).

The purpose that the devil and his demons have for lying is to deceive. Those who listen to their lies stand in danger of believing what they say. The speaking of demons is never motivated by a desire to help us; the demons are laying snares. For us to listen to them with the intention of sorting out any truth that they might utter, could be compared to drinking water with poison in it with an intention of filtering out the poison with our teeth.

3. God is a jealous God. We must not look to any other spirit for guidance, knowledge, wisdom, healing or power. "For Jehovah thy God is a devouring fire, a jealous God" (Deuteronomy 4:24). If we need to know anything about the activity of the enemy, we must go to God rather than rely upon the enemy.

Joshua, the leader of God's army, created an irreversible problem when he sought guidance by the interrogation of the enemy instead of seeking the Lord. The account is found in the ninth chapter of Joshua.

During the conquest of Caanan, the Gibeonites sent an ambassage to Joshua, posing as representatives of a far country. Although they were the next people in the line of Israel's conquest, they craftily disguised themselves as travelers from a distant land and deceived Joshua into making a covenant of non-aggression with them. God's Word declares, "And the men [of Israel] took of their provision, AND ASKED NOT COUNSEL AT THE MOUTH OF JEHOVAH" (Joshua 9:14).

4. We have access to all truth and all power in and through the Holy Spirit.[11] We are in no way dependent upon Satan's lies and half truths. Any supposed help an evil spirit might give us can be obtained through the Holy Spirit. Which of these two sources of gaining knowledge glorifies God? Which is the wisest course to follow?

5. Depending upon demons for information discourages the use of the gifts of the Holy Spirit. "Desire earnestly the greater gifts" (I Corinthians 12:31). "Follow after love; yet desire earnestly spiritual gifts" (I Corinthians 14:1). The One who has called us to warfare will equip us for warfare. We should eagerly desire the power gifts of the Holy Spirit. These gifts increase by faith and by use.

---

11 John 8:31-32; I Corinthians 12:7-11.

The gifts of the Spirit most often needed for casting out demons are: the word of knowledge, the word of wisdom, the gift of faith and the gift of discerning of spirits. These spiritual gifts come to us through "the promise of the Father" (Acts 1:4), the empowerment of the Holy Spirit. "But ye shall receive power, when the Holy Spirit is come upon you..." (Acts 1:8).

6. Relying upon demons allows them to direct the ministry. We must allow the Holy Spirit to lead the way and not permit demons to control or influence a deliverance session. If we rely upon a demon to give us information about himself or about other indwelling spirits, we are handing the reins of mininstry over to that demon. The battle plan is then determined by what the evil spirits tell us. In every ministry the Holy Spirit must be our Guide. When information given by demons is used to guide a ministry, then demons are taking the place that only the Holy Spirit should fill.

7. There is no scriptural basis for conversing with demons. In fact, conversing with demons is forbidden by Scripture. "There shall not be found with thee any one that (is) a consulter with a familiar spirit....or (is) a necromancer" (Deuteronomy 18:10-11). In other words, those who consult with a familiar spirit or, through necromancy, attempt to communicate with the dead, actually communicate with demons.

Note: In Mark 5:9 Jesus asked the demon speaking through the Gadarene demoniac, "What is your name?" Why did Jesus command Legion to name himself? Was Jesus ignorant as to Legion's identity? No, Jesus knows all things. His knowledge is complete. Was information as to the identity of Legion necessary to the man's deliverance? No, Jesus did not utilize Legion's identity in setting the man free. Then, we must look elsewhere for the answer as to why Jesus commanded Legion to reveal his identity.

When Jesus began commanding and questioning the demon, the evil spirit reacted; "And crying out with a loud voice, he said...I solemnly implore you by God, do not begin to torment me!" (Mark 5:7, Amplified). When a demon is forced to identify himself, it causes that spirit to lose his power. So, the questioning was not to gain information, but was a tactic of spiritual warfare. Demons are best able to do their work when they can conceal their presence and identity. They work under a cover of darkness. It is a severe blow to them when their presence and nature is revealed. To force a demon to disclose himself is a major step toward casting him out. This is a useful tactic when confronting obstinate and tenacious demons.

Note: Another very plausible explanation of Mark 5:9 is that Jesus asked the man (not the demon) his name. The purpose would have been to bring the man back into control of his faculties. Such a procedure is common practice among deliverance ministers in cases where demons dominate a person. But the answer came from the indwelling demon, not from the man, giving the name "Legion"

8. It prolongs the deliverance and is inconsiderate of the person receiving deliverance. As long as a demon can distract a deliverance minister through his speaking, he is postponing his eviction with a ruse by which he hopes to escape. Also, it is very de-edifying to the person through whom demons speak. Persons through whom demons have spoken are usually left with a feeling of confusion and defilement. On the other hand, The Holy Spirit speaks through a person unto edification: "He that speaks in tongues edifies himself" (II Cor. 14:4). A second way in which the Holy Spirit speaks through a person is by prophecy, and prophetic utterance is uplifting: "Everyone who prophesies speaks to men for their strengthening, encouragement and comfort...he who prophesies edifies the church" (I Corinthians 14:3, 4b NIV). The evil spirit's influence is the opposite. The Holy Spirit speaks only through a yielded vessel, but the evil spirit controls a person's speech.

9. We must flee the temptation to pride by boasting that we have conversed with demons. Pride is the sin which caused the devil to lose his favor with God, and he tempts every person with pride.[12] If the devil can cause a

---

12 Isaiah 14:12-15; Ezekiel 28:15-17; I Timothy 3:6.

deliverance minister to fall into pride, even the pride of having conversed with demons, he has laid a successful snare for that man's feet. One is never made strong by contemplating what demons have told him, but one becomes strong as a tree planted by streams of water when he dwells upon what God has said.[13] Success over the enemy comes through reciting God's Word and meditating upon it day and night. God said to Joshua as he faced the giants of Canaan land:

> This book of the law shall not depart out of thy mouth, but thou shalt meditate thereon day and night, that thou mayest observe to do according to all that is written therein; for then thou shalt make thy way prosperous, and then thou shalt have good success.
>
> Joshua 1:8

10. We must flee from the deception of thinking that we have received private and valuable information from demons. The devil knows quite well that anyone who adds to or takes away from what is written in the Bible is brought under a curse. God's Word ends with this sober warning:

> I testify unto every man that heareth the words of the prophecy of this book, If any man shall add unto them, God shall add unto him the plagues which are written in this book; and if any man shall take away from the words of the book of this prophecy, God shall take away his part from the tree of life, and out of the holy city, which are written in this book.
>
> Revelation 22:18-19

If one communicates with evil spirits, he may become convinced that he has gained special information about the devil's hierarchy, the devil's plans, or other revelation knowledge. If a person accepts such information and teaches it as truth, then he has fallen into deception. The

---

13 See: Psalm 1:1-3.

Bible warns us that such deceptions will occur in the latter days.

> The Spirit clearly says that in later times some will abandon the faith and follow deceiving spirits and things taught by demons.
>
> I Timothy 4:1 NIV

11. Conversing with demons is not necessary for a person's deliverance. Jesus cast out demons without conversing with them, and so do effective deliverance ministers today.

12. Demon speaking does not promote faith. It might be theorized that hearing demons speak will produce faith in skeptics and those not yet convinced that demons are real. The Bible does not teach that faith comes by hearing demons speak, but that "Faith comes from hearing the message, and the message is heard through the word of Christ" (Romans 10:17 NIV).

Demon talk can excite the flesh, but in itself it has no useful purpose. In the New Testament demons sometimes spoke and cried out when being expelled; also, today's deliverance minister may experience the same, but one must refrain from seeking a thrill or gaining information through encouraging demons to talk.

13. Conversing with demons can easily lead to the forbidden role of being a "consulter with familiar spirits" (Deuteronomy 18:11). If one becomes a communication link with the demonic realm, he becomes a spiritist medium, and the information he transmits is a "doctrine that demons teach" (I Timothy 4:1 NIV). Thus, interrogation of demons and conversation with them is not only foolish but exceedingly dangerous.

Demon Resistance

Evil spirits resist being cast out. This is what is meant by the phrase "tearing him" regarding the man in Capernaum (Mark 1:26). Manifestations accompanying deliverance are, in some instances, demonstrations of resistance. It seems as though the demon is determined to do as much damage as he can before he departs. Occasionally a person is thrown down, contorted, stricken with pain or left with an acute weakness in the wake of deliverance.

If permitted or encouraged to do so, demons will often manifest themselves demonstratively. If demons are bound and prohibited by spiritual authority from manifesting unnecessarily, there is a noticeable lessening of their activity. Nevertheless, any valid ministry of deliverance can anticipate some manifestations. Since Jesus did not curtail all manifestations, then neither should we expect to do so.

Manifestations

Demon manifestations turn some people on and turn others off. It is unscriptural either to revel in manifestations or to be repulsed by them. In the passage in Mark 1, the spirit "cried out" when it was initially flushed up, and again "crying with a loud voice" as it was being cast out. Other common manifestations are: coughing and retching (sometimes with phlegm and occasionally with blood, but seldom with vomit), burping, yawning, sighing, crying and laughing. However,

> manifestations must not become the criteria by which successful deliverance is judged.

Some persons receive very valid deliverance without any perceptible manifestations, so it is error to require manifestations as evidence of deliverance. Encouraging demons to manifest gives them license to become demonstrative and violent. The following account is a typical example:

Our ministry team was conducting a group deliverance session in Switzerland. A certain man began to forcefully strike the back of the seat in front of him with his fists as though it were a punching bag. As one of our counselors began to command the spirits out, the man fell to the floor and began to gnaw the deliverance counselor's boot. After several minutes of violent struggle, the demons were expelled and the brother was set free. Upon questioning the fellow we learned that he had been told that manifestations were necessary to his deliverance; therefore, he had yielded to the spirits in him so as to give them permission to manifest.

In the practice of spiritism and witchcraft, demons are courted and their manifestations are welcomed, whereupon they will perform amazing and bizarre feats. Likewise, in deliverance situations where demon manifestations are sought by the deliverance minister, the demons will comply with such things as talking through the person, controlling the person's body, causing the person to become violent and destructive, or by immobilizing the person as though he were unconscious or dead.

Demons are prideful by nature and love to take the center of attention. Why encourage demons to show off bad behavior? Why not uplift Jesus in every way and cause Him to be glorified in the midst of the battle?

> The goal in deliverance should be to cast the spirit out in the shortest time possible with the least possible demonstration.

This conserves the energy of the deliverance minister, shows regard for the person receiving deliverance, glorifies God and brings better over-all results.

Reactions To Deliverance

People have varied reactions to deliverance. In Mark 1:27 some of the people of Capernaum were amazed and questioned among themselves. They appreciated the fact of the man's deliverance but puzzled over the ease and authority with which it was accomplished. Such astonishment is a common reaction from persons experiencing or witnessing deliverance for the first time. Two thousand years later people are still prone to question: "What is this? a new teaching!" (Mark 1:27).

27

The answers to the "what's" of deliverance are not to be found within oneself but in the Word of God. Some, through human logic, have concluded that deliverance is a mere illusion, hypnotism, demonic trickery or staged performance. If these conclusions were true, the ministry of Jesus would be invalidated; instead, His ministry verifies today's deliverance experiences.

Authority Over Demons

> New Testament deliverance is accomplished by spiritual authority.

Jesus has authority in Himself and has given it to His followers.

> And Jesus came to them and spake unto them, saying, All authority hath been given unto me in heaven and on earth. Go ye therefore...
>
> Matthew 28:18,19a

When Jesus cast an unclean spirit out of the man in the synagogue it created quite a stir. Now, the people in Jesus's day were familiar with demon spirits. The Jews in the synagogue did not for a moment question the reality of demons nor the fact that the man in their midst had demons in him. (Some today have not yet progressed this far in their understanding.) But what puzzled the Jews was the authority that Jesus demonstrated, which was in marked contrast to their own methods of exorcism.

In absolute amazement they said, "With authority he commandeth even the unclean spirits, and they do obey him" (Mark 1:27 KJ). His demonstration of authority was as startling to those in the synagogue as it was to his chosen twelve when He commanded winds and waves to be calm.

The methods of exorcism employed by the Jews in the days of Jesus paralleled those of the heathen peoples who used superstitious incantations, magic formulas and herbal concoctions. The ancient historian, Josephus, tells of exorcisms that he personally witnessed performed by one Eleazar, who claimed to have acquired his abilities from wisdom passed down by Solomon. If, indeed, his methods did come from Solomon, Solomon surely derived his techniques from his heathen wives and concubines when he was an old man and had forsaken the ways of God.

Josephus describes one of the rites of exorcism performed by Eleazar: "The manner of the cure was this: He put a ring that had a root of one of those sorts mentioned by Solomon to the nostrils of the demoniac, after which he drew out the demon through his nostrils: and when the man fell down immediately, he adjured him to return into him no more, making still mention of Solomon, and reciting the incantations which he composed."[14]

Rev. Alfred Edersheim, the English scholar, also recites some of the bizarre techniques and incantations employed by Jewish exorcists. He concludes his article by stating: "It has been a weary and unpleasant task to record such abject superstitions...Greater contrast could scarcely be conceived than between what we read in the New Testament and the views and practices mentioned in Rabbinic writings — and if this, as is hoped, has been firmly established, even the ungrateful labour bestowed on collecting these unsavoury notices will have been sufficiently repaid."[15]

The account of the vagabond exorcists in Acts 19 is given in such a way as to contrast their miserable failure with Paul's success in casting out demons.

> But certain also of the strolling Jews, exorcists, took upon them to name over them that had the evil spirits the name of the Lord Jesus, saying, I adjure you by Jesus whom Paul preacheth...And the evil spirits answered and said unto them, Jesus I know, and Paul I know; but who are ye? And the man in whom the evil spirit was leaped on

---

14 Josephus, *Antiquities of the Jews*,VIII, 5.
15 Edersheim, *The Life and Times of Jesus the Messiah*, p.776.

them, and mastered both of them, and prevailed against them, so that they fled out of that house naked and wounded.

Acts 19:13,15-16

The Sons of Sceva surely learned from their sobering experience that parroting the Name of Jesus carried no authority. Only true believers in Christ have the right to use His Name.

Although both the vagabond exorcists and Paul used spoken words as their method of addressing evil spirits; the Jews used superstitious incantations while the disciple of Jesus employed words of true spiritual authority.

The method of deliverance that distinguished both Jesus and His disciples from all others was "authority". This fact comes to light in Mark 1:27 when the Jews in the synagogue marveled, "With authority he commandeth even the unclean spirits, and they obey him".

The one thing that Jesus consistently bestowed upon His disciples was "authority" to cast out demons. When the twelve were commissioned He, "gave them authority over unclean spirits, to cast them out" (Matthew 10:1); "...that he might send them forth to preach, and to have authority to cast out demons" (Mark 3:14-15).

When the seventy appointees returned from their first mission they reported, "even the demons are subject unto us in thy name" (Luke 10:17). The verb "subject" is a military term describing subjection and obedience to authority. When the disciples commanded the demons to "go", they went!

Jesus reminded the seventy that they should not be surprised that demons submitted to their authority: "Behold, I have given you authority...over all the power of the enemy" (Luke 10:19).

How is authority implemented? Jesus "commanded" demons with authority. Authority is administered through direct commands.

> The biblical method of deliverance is to "cast out demons" by commanding them to go in the name of Jesus! (Mark 16:17).

When deliverance from demons is needed, one must not seek alternatives to casting them out with authority. For example, demons cannot be counseled out. Counseling should accompany deliverance, but counseling is not deliverance. Also, spiritual growth is vital and will lessen the influence of demons, but even maturing in Christ is not an alternative to deliverance. Suppressed spirits are content to wait for some future opportunity to spring back into action.

> Deliverance requires no material paraphernalia.

Spiritual authority is not co-dependant upon a Bible laid on the counselee's body, a cross or crucifix placed on his chest, communion wine poured down his throat or holy water sprinkled on his head. The name of Jesus is our authority, and in His name we employ our spiritual weapons. We wield the "sword of the Spirit" as we read and quote scriptures; we utilize the power in Christ's blood when we testify of its power to justify, redeem, atone and cleanse; we overcome the devil through "the word of our testimony" when we testify that Jesus Christ is the Son of God who came in the flesh, lived without sin, died on the cross to bear the penalty for our sins, was resurrected from the dead, ascended into heaven and is coming again in His glory to judge the world.

The Minister's Reputation

"And the report of him went out straightway everywhere into all the region...round about" (Mark 1:28). Deliverance ministers quickly develop a reputation. Persons will hear the reports and come from far and wide to receive this ministry. There are many desperate persons who have been tormented by demons for so long that they welcome the news of help and press forward to receive it.

One thing a deliverance minister never needs is publicity. He never needs to advertise his ministry because everyone he helps will tell others and he will soon have more persons knocking at his door than he has time or strength to help. This enables us to understand why Jesus sometimes told those healed and delivered through His ministry not to tell anyone else. He needed time with the twelve to teach and train them.

> People are so desperate and needy that the deliverance minister sometimes must guard his time for other important matters.

It was because of the press of the crowd that Jesus told His disciples to pray that the Lord would send out more laborers. This is also why Jesus Himself trained and sent out the twelve and the seventy. One man, not even Jesus in the flesh, could minister to all who needed it.[16]

> Those called by God into deliverance ministry will do well to follow the example of Jesus in spending part of their time in training others.

In the long run, more people will receive deliverance as new workers are trained and sent into the field.

---

16 Matthew 9:32-10:8.

DELIVERANCE
IN THE ATONEMENT

Mark 1:32-34; **Matthew 8:16-17;** Luke 4:40-41

16 And when even was come, they brought unto
him many possessed with demons: and he
cast out the spirits with a word, and healed all

17 that were sick: that it might be fulfilled which
was spoken through Isaiah the prophet, saying, Himself took our infirmities, and bare our
diseases.

Here is proof that Jesus died for the whole man: spirit,
soul and body. The great Messianic prophecy of Isaiah
53:4 is declared fulfilled through Jesus's ministry of deliverance and healing. Isaiah chapter fifty-three foretells
God's provision for sinful man through the atoning work
of the Messiah.

He was despised, and rejected of men; a man of sorrows,
and acquainted with grief: and as one from whom men hide
their face he was despised; and we esteemed him not. Surely
he hath borne our griefs, and carried our sorrows: yet we did
esteem him stricken, smitten of God, and afflicted. But he
was wounded for our transgressions, he was bruised for our
iniquities; the chastisement of our peace was upon him; and
with his stripes we were healed. All we like sheep have gone
astray; we have turned everyone to his own way; and
Jehovah hath laid on him the iniquity of us all.

Isaiah 53:3-5

What a provision! Our Lord Jesus Christ took upon Himself the penalty of sin due to us. He rescued us from spiritual death through His physical death, and through His suffering we have healing and deliverance for body and soul.

Benefits Of The Cross

In other words, there is provision in the cross for more than the gift of eternal life. Large segments of the church have been taught that the new birth is the only benefit of His suffering and death. However, sin not only brought death to the human spirit, but it brought weaknesses and infirmities to the body and soul as well.

The benefits of the cross are to be appropriated in the ways which God has prescribed. The total provisions of the cross do not come automatically with the new birth experience. If this were true, no Christian would ever be physically sick, for "by his stripes we were healed" (I Peter 2:24). There are ways to appropriate physical healing. Sometimes there are prerequisites to meet before healing comes. Also, whenever demons are responsible for a man's sickness of body or personality, the demons must be cast out. By faith in Jesus as the Son of God and Savior, and by faith to command demons in His name, demons are cast out. It is active, obedient faith that drives out evil spirits. The Word does not instruct us to believe that God will take away our demons but that we are given authority over them ourselves.

Why Command A Demon More Than Once?

"He cast out the spirits with a word" (Matthew 8:16). If Jesus cast out demons with one word of command, why cannot we always do the same? Upon close examination we find that this passage does not actually teach that Jesus cast out demons with one word.

It is a widespread error of belief that Jesus never commanded an evil spirit more than once. However, there is no article in the Greek text. The verse literally says: "He cast out the spirits *with word*." The Greek construction places the emphasis upon the authority expressed by spoken word.

In contrast to the Jewish exorcists, who used incantations, herbs and occult paraphernalia, Jesus simply spoke authoritatively to demons and they obeyed Him. In the case of the Gadarene, Jesus commanded the demon repeatedly. In the Greek, the verb "said" (Mark 5:8) expresses continuous action which is translated by the Amplified Bible: "For Jesus *was commanding*. Come out of the man, you unclean spirit!" (Mark 5:8). Literally, Jesus was commanding over and over, "Come out of him! Come out of him! Come out of him"!

Demons are personalities. Like people, some unclean spirits are stronger willed than others and, therefore, slower to respond to orders given. Too, our warfare against demon spirits is a wrestling conflict whereby continuous pressure is placed upon them until they are defeated. Repeated commands given to demons keeps spiritual pressure upon them until they yield.

We are not to suppose that commanding a demon more than once is a negative reflection upon our faith but rather a witness to the quality of our faith. True faith is persistent and active, not presumptuous and passive.

MINISTERING TO THE MULTITUDE

Mark 3:8-15

8 A great multitude, hearing what great things

9 he did, came unto him. And he spake to his disciples, that a little boat should wait on him because of the crowd, lest they should throng

10 him, for he had healed many; insomuch that as many as had plagues pressed upon him

11 that they might touch him. And the unclean spirits, whensoever they beheld him, fell down before him, and cried, saying, Thou art

12 the Son of God. And he charged them much

13 that they should not make him known. And he goeth up into the mountain, and calleth unto him whom he himself would: and they

14 went unto him. And he appointed twelve, that they might be with him, and that he might

15 send them forth to preach, and to have authority to cast out demons.

The more Jesus ministered to the needs of the people the more they pressed in. He found it expedient to get in a boat and minister just off the shore of the Sea of Galilee to prevent the people from thronging Him. They pressed upon Him just to touch him. The evil spirits in those within the crowd reacted to the very presence of the Son of God. From this account we learn that:

1. Unclean spirits readily recognized Jesus as the Son of God while the Jewish nation as a whole could not decide upon His true identity. The demons had one advantage which men did not possess, for they knew that He was sinless. All their efforts to cause Him to sin had failed.

2. Unclean spirits are forced to bow before Jesus. Here they "fell down before Him." Their acknowledgment was more than recognition: it was surrender.[17]

3. Unclean spirits can be kept from speaking. Jesus charged them not to make Him known. Even when spirits speak truth, their testimony is not to be received. As important as it is for men to know who Jesus is, in order to believe in Him, the testimony of demons is not valid. Jesus consistently refused to accept any witness of Himself that came from demons.

Demons also recognize the anointed servants of God. They replied to the sons of Sceva, "Jesus I know and Paul I know about, but who are you?" (Acts 19:15 NIV).

Just as evil spirits recoiled from Jesus' authority over them, they also tremble when confronted by Christian warriors who walk in discernment and faith.

From time to time reports have come through other deliverance ministers that they have heard demons say they knew the Hammonds. One pastor said, "I have been talking with a demon, and I asked him about you. Would you like to know what that demon thought about you?" I was repulsed by the question! Without hesitation I replied, "I have no interest in what demons think about me; all I'm interested in is what the Lord thinks about me."

Wisdom dictates that we totally reject what evil spirits have to say. To do otherwise puts one in peril of the devil's snare of pride and deception.

---

17 Philippians 2:9-11.

> Any truth demons speak is intended to en-
> snare and never has a beneficial effect.

4. Jesus chose disciples and prepared them to continue His ministry. What was His ministry? Jesus answered this question for us when He stood in the synagogue in Nazareth and read concerning Himself from the prophet Isaiah:

> The Spirit of the Lord is upon me,
> Because he anointed me to preach good
>   tidings to the poor:
> He hath sent me to proclaim release to
>   the captives,
> And recovering of sight to the blind,
> To set at liberty them that are bruised,
> To proclaim the acceptable year of the Lord.
>
> Luke 4:18-19

The work of deliverance today is a continuation of Jesus' ministry. Therefore, deliverance remains as much a part of the Church's commission as does preaching, teaching and healing.

CONTINUED MINISTRY TO THE MULTITUDES

Luke 6:17-19

17 And he came down with them, and stood on a level place, and a great multitude of his disciples, and a great number of the people from all Judaea and Jerusalem, and the sea coast of Tyre and Sidon, who came to hear him,

18 and to be healed of their diseases; and they that were troubled with unclean spirits were

19 healed. And all the multitude sought to touch him; for power came forth from him, and healed them all.

This account seems to parallel the occasion of the Sermon on the Mount found in Matthew 5-7. Only Luke's account relates Jesus' ministry of healing and deliverance to his disciples, plus a great number of people from various locales.

The ones delivered of unclean spirits are said to have been troubled (vexed, harassed or disturbed) by them. These synonyms accurately describe the effects of evil spirits within one's life. On the one hand, Jesus is the Prince of Peace and His Lordship produces peace in His disciples; on the other hand, the devil is a peace destroyer. The absence of peace and the presence of troubling is indicative of demonization.

The Greek word *ochleo* translated "vexed" in the King James translation is also found in Acts 5:16: "There came also a multitude out of the cities round about unto Jerusalem, bringing sick folks, and them which were vexed with unclean spirits: and they were healed every one."

After Christ's Ascension, the ministry of deliverance continued through the ministry of the apostles and spread through new disciples. Deliverance ministry continues today, and by the grace of God is being fully restored to the body of Christ.

"Soteria", the word *salvation* in Greek, means *deliverance*. Therefore, the full gospel of salvation includes not only the good news of deliverance from the penalty of sin but also the good news of deliverance from the power of unclean spirits and diseases. The gospel is the good news of all the blessings bestowed by God on men in Christ through the Holy Spirit.

PRAYER FOR DELIVERANCE

Matthew 6:13

13 And bring us not into temptation, but deliver
us from the evil one.

This familiar excerpt from the Lord's Prayer teaches us
to pray daily for deliverance. We need God's continuous
protection from the devil, especially from his temptations.
In Matthew 26:41 Jesus warned His disciples, "watch and
pray, that ye enter not into temptation." They failed to
heed His warning due to weakness of the flesh and conse-
quently were not prepared to cope with the testings that
came. For example: Peter denied the Lord; they all followed afar off; they became discouraged, returned to their
fishing, and doubted the first reports of His resurrection.
Jesus had previously warned that Satan desired to have
them and sift them as wheat. Satan desires to sift each of
us, too.

> Through unceasing prayer we remain vigilant;
> therefore, prayerlessness is deadly to Christian
> life, for it permits the devil to move in.

THE TEST OF
TRUE DISCIPLESHIP

Matthew 7:21-23; Luke 6:46

21 Not every one that saith unto me, Lord, Lord,
shall enter the kingdom of heaven; but he
that doeth the will of my Father who is in

22 heaven. Many will say to me in that day,
Lord, Lord, did we not prophesy by thy name,
and by thy name cast out demons, and by thy

23 name do many mighty works? And then will I
profess unto them, I never knew you: depart
from me, ye that work iniquity.

Here is a serious warning couched in the strongest of
language. Not everybody that's talking about heaven is
going there! This warning is addressed to some who say,
"Lord, Lord" and claim worthiness on the grounds of their
supernatural works (casting out of demons included). On
the day of judgment Jesus will say to many of these, "I
never knew you: depart from me, ye that work iniquity."

Two important lessons should be learned from the context of Matthew 7:13-23. First, the warning is real! The
application of the warning is to:

(1) Those who have not entered the path of eternal life through the straight and narrow gate
by repentance from sin and faith in the Lord
Jesus Christ (v.13-14);

(2) False prophets whose fruits of character do
not measure up to their profession of Christ's
Lordship (v.15-16);

(3) Those who call Him "Lord" but who fail to do the Father's will (v.21); and

(4) Those who claim supernatural works done by His name as sole merit for His acceptance (v.22)

All of the above are identified as workers of "iniquity" who will be irreversibly rejected by Christ "in that day" of final judgment, and whose fate is to be "hewn down and cast into the fire".

This passage enforces the doctrine of salvation by grace through faith and not by works.[18] The primary consideration for every man should be the matter of his eternal destiny. Otherwise, all a person's good works are vain.

Furthermore, even miracles performed in the name of Jesus provide no basis for rejoicing. When the seventy newly-appointed disciples began to rejoice over their deliverance victories, Jesus brought them back into balance through these words:

> In this rejoice not, that the spirits are subject unto you; but rejoice that your names are written in heaven,
>
> Luke 10:20.

Second, some who are genuinely saved are tormented by Christ's warnings of damnation. They live in fear of ultimate rejection. In spite of their faith in Christ and years of faithful service they tremble at the thought of judgment, feeling certain of their Lord's ultimate condemnation: "I never knew you: depart from me, ye that work iniquity" (Matthew 7:23).

What makes some Christians so fearful of judgment? They are not perfected in love. They obviously have been neglected, rejected and abused by other people; therefore, they remain unsure of love — even the love of God. But...

> God is love; and he that abideth in love abideth in God, and God abideth in him. Herein is love made perfect with us, that we may have boldness in the day of judgment,
>
> I John 4:16-17.

---

18 See: Ephesians 2:8,9.

Sometimes a guilt root is responsible for the tormenting fear of judgment in a born-again person. Although he has asked God's forgiveness, the devil continues to accuse him and make him feel unworthy of forgiveness. Actually, no one is worthy of forgiveness. Forgiveness is ours by the grace of God. As long as a believer permits the devil to condemn him, his peace will be destroyed and he will have no assurance that God will answer his prayers. Furthermore, he will be sidelined in spiritual warfare. How can he cast out a demon when he is so conscious of his sin?

How can one ever be sure that he is forgiven and will not be among the ultimately rejected? Simple! Meet God's conditions of repentance and faith and walk in obedience. Then believe what God has said:

> If we confess our sins, he is faithful and righteous to forgive us our sins, and to cleanse us from all unrighteousness,
>
> I John 1:9.

Some who lack understanding and appreciation of the ministry of deliverance have twisted the scriptures by asserting that all who cast out demons, especially out of Christians, ultimately will be damned. Such critics grossly err in their contention that all deliverance ministers are false and disapproved by God. We are not intimidated by such absurd charges, for we know our Lord's commission to cast out demons. Let the critics examine the fruit, for "a tree is known by its fruit" (Matthew 12:33b).

This sort of attack upon Christ's servants is a Satanic tactic to divert the minister of deliverance from his work into a defense of his ministry. The Scribes and Pharisees were unsuccessful in their attempts to sidetrack Jesus with such tactics. Jesus briefly pointed out their error and went right on ministering to those who welcomed Him. This is a safe and fruitful course for Christ's disciples to follow today.

THE TESTIMONY OF MIRACLES

Luke 7:21

21 In that hour he cured many of diseases and plagues and evil spirits; and on many that were blind he bestowed sight.

In this context John the Baptist has questioned the Messiahship of Jesus. John is imprisoned and sends a delegation to ask, "Art thou he that cometh, or look we for another?" (Luke 7:19) Jesus instructed the delegation from John to report on His supernatural works. Jesus was fulfilling all that had been prophesied concerning His ministry.[19]

Jesus did not condemn John the Baptist for questioning His identity; on the contrary, he proceeded to pay John the loftiest eulogy ever uttered. The Lord always met sincere inquiry with sincere answers, while His unteachable critics received His "woes."

Every minister of the Gospel is subject to questioning and criticism as to his doctrine, his authority and the validity of his ministry. In humility the man of God should realize that he is not beyond error. Wisdom dictates that one remain open to correction. Criticism can be constructive; it can deliver a person out of error and deception. Defensiveness and sensitiveness render one unable to evaluate criticism and accept correction.

19 Isaiah 29:18,19; 35:5,6; 61:11.

My wife and I have had many opportunities to relate to criticism. When our book, *Pigs In The Parlor* was published, it contained a chapter on "Proxy Deliverance". A minister from South Africa advised us that this teaching was wrong and that he could not recommend our book because of this one chapter. I became defensive and refused his criticism. Later, the Lord dealt with my heart, and I saw that the term "proxy" did not convey what we really intended to say. "Proxy" carries the idea that one can stand in for another person. This was interpreted by some to mean that a proxy can invite into himself the demons which indwell another person and then receive deliverance for the other person.

In a subsequent printing of *Pigs In The Parlor*, the chapter on "Proxy Deliverance" was changed to "Intercessory Prayer Warfare". However, this revision opened the door for new objections, and a few people reproved us for changing the chapter. Nevertheless, we were thankful for the constructive criticism that helped us correct something that did not convey what we intended and was causing some to err. Most deliverance workers agree that it is unscriptural and dangerous for a person to invite demons into himself for any reason whatsoever, even though his intentions are beneficent.

If God's servant knows who he is in Christ, knows His calling, knows that he is in God's will, knows that he is grounded in the Word and produces good fruit then doubters and critics will not move him from his confidence.

I recall an incident when my ministry was challenged. At the conclusion of a teaching, a young man leaped to the platform with an open Bible shouting at me for having said that I ministered deliverance to believers. When he finally calmed down a little, I reminded him that Jesus commissioned believers to cast out demons. I quoted Mark 16:17 which states that those who believe shall cast out demons. If he was not casting demons out of Christians then out of whom was he casting them? He had no answer, for he was not casting demons out of anyone.

When criticism is unfounded, the fruit of one's ministry is answer enough. When the Pharisees accused Jesus of casting out demons by the power of Beelzebub, He responded, "Either make the tree good, and its fruit good; or make the tree corrupt, and its fruit corrupt: for the tree is known by its fruit" (Matthew 12:33).

Nevertheless, even good fruit will not satisfy those who are blinded by their own prejudices. Even Jesus, the Master Teacher, was unable to satisfy the minds of the unteachable. Furthermore, they refused to acknowledge the "good fruit" of His deliverance ministry.

The Pharisees and scribes also accused John the Baptist of having a demon because he came neither eating nor drinking. These same individuals turned right around and accused Jesus of being a glutton and a winebibber because He came eating and drinking.[20]

The scripture says, "But the Pharisees and the lawyers rejected for themselves the counsel of God..." Luke 7:30.

If John the Baptist and Jesus were falsely accused and criticized, can other of God's servants expect better treatment?

Men who are blinded by prideful religious legalism or bound by dead religious traditionalism cannot discern the true nature of the Kingdom of God nor rightly divide the word of truth. To such critics Jesus replied, "Yet wisdom is justified and vindicated by what she does (her deeds) and by her children" (Matthew 11:19b, Amplified Bible). In other words, inspect the fruit!

---

20 Matthew 11:18, 19; Luke 7:33, 34.

HEALED OF DEMONS

Luke 8:1-3

1 And it came to pass soon afterwards, that he went about through cities and villages, preaching and bringing the good tidings of the kingdom of God, and with him the twelve,

2 and certain women which had been healed of evil spirits and infirmities: Mary that was called Magdalene, from whom seven demons

3 had gone out, and Joanna the wife of Chuzas Herod's steward, and Susanna, and many others, who ministered unto them of their substance.

Cities and Villages

Jesus did not restrict Himself to large ministries, but was found showing His compassion in both the cities and in the villages. Traveling ministers will have opportunity to follow the example of Jesus. Why minister to a handful of people when one can minister to thousands? Here is where one must walk in the counsel of the Holy Spirit. Philip, the deacon-evangelist, was having a very successful ministry in Samaria when the Spirit bid him leave there and go into the desert region and minister to one man, the Ethiopian eunuch. Who knows the spiritual influence this servant of a queen carried back to his own country? We must not assume that the Lord would have us limit ministry to large cities or large congregations.

The Full Gospel

Once again we see that the gospel of the Kingdom included healing and deliverance. This is what some call "the full gospel." Any gospel that does not include the full benefits of the cross must be considered a partial gospel.

Training Others

Jesus had the twelve with him, for He was training these men to carry out His ministry after His departure. Whatever ministries are given unto us, the Lord would have us train others to be assistants, extensions and inheritors of that ministry. "And the things that thou hast heard from me among many witnesses, the same commit thou to faithful men, who shall be able to teach others also" (II Tim. 2:2).

Healing The Personality

The word "heal" is not limited to physical healing, but it is applied also in the New Testament to healing of the human spirit and soul (personality). In this text certain women received a twofold healing. We can safely assume that each of them had already received the healing of their spirits, which resulted in salvation unto eternal life. Persons may experience spiritual new birth and still need healing in their physical bodies and personalities. All healing does not come in one package.

Specifically, these women were healed of "evil spirits and infirmities." Since the healing from evil spirits was distinct from the healing of infirmities, it obviously was a healing of something other than their bodies. The only other facet of their beings that could need healing would be their souls (Greek: psuche) or selves. The self, or personality, is expressed through thoughts, emotions and will. These are the most common areas of demonic bondage. Many Christians are bound in their personalities; therefore, they are unstable souls.[21]

There are four different words in the Greek New

---

21 II Peter 2:24; James 1:8.

Testament translated "heal" or "healing". The word used in this text is *therapeuo*, from which we derive the English word "therapy." This word describes the care and attendance necessary to bring a person back to wholeness. It describes a process of healing unto which a person is committed until the therapist has completed the work of rehabilitation. This word accurately conveys the truth that one's deliverance may entail a period of time before the deliverance is complete. This time process is not due to the length of time it requires to cast out spirits, but the time that it takes for the person to become self-disciplined and to fill his "house" with the things of God.

The picture we get from *therapeuo* is of these women continuing to submit to the ministry of Jesus until they finally came into stability of personality and wholeness of body. If they had become discouraged over the time factor, they would never have known the victory.

Seven Demons

Mary Magdalene was delivered of "seven spirits." We are led to question why the number of spirits is given. Almost any deliverance minister will tell you that it is not unusual to cast scores and hundreds of demons out of a person. The Gadarene demoniac had a "legion" of spirits which would be upward of five thousand! What could be so noteworthy about Mary Magdalene's having seven spirits? The impression left is that she was extensively demonized. This explanation must be labeled as theoretical, but Mary probably had seven ruler spirits (strong men) who in turn were leaders over multitudes of other spirits. Each ruler spirit could easily have represented seven different demonic personalities. Hers would then be a case of severe demonization worthy of special mention.

Free To Serve

Those who have been set free are so grateful that they are eager to bless those who were used of God to accomplish their deliverance. These women gave of themselves and their means to minister to Jesus and the twelve. Their hearts overflowed with love. Can't you imagine the work involved in feeding and doing the laundry for thirteen robust, active men?

Individuals who are continually aware of their own problems are unable to serve others. One of the greatest blessings of breaking the bondages within self is the liberty to serve others. Since the Body of Christ is to be a serving organism, its various members must be free in order for it to accomplish its ministry.

TWO OPPOSING KINGDOMS

Mark 3:22-30; **Matthew 12:22-37**

22 Then was brought unto him one possessed with a demon, blind and dumb: and he healed him, insomuch that the dumb man

23 spake and saw. And all the multitudes were amazed, and said, Can this be the son of

24 David? But when the Pharisees heard it, they said, This man doth not cast out demons, but

25 by Beelzebub the prince of the demons. And knowing their thoughts he said unto them, Every kingdom divided against itself is brought to desolation; and every city or house

26 divided against itself shall not stand: and if Satan casteth out Satan, he is divided against himself; how then shall his kingdom stand?

27 And if I by Beelzebub cast out demons, by whom do your sons cast them out? therefore

28 shall they be your judges. But if I by the Spirit of God cast out demons, then is the

29 kingdom of God come upon you. Or how can one enter into the house of the strong man, and spoil his goods, except he first bind the strong man? and then he will spoil his house.

30 He that is not with me is against me; and he
31 that gathereth not with me scattereth. There-

fore I say unto you, Every sin and blasphemy
shall be forgiven unto men; but the blasphemy against the Spirit shall not be forgiven.

32 And whosoever shall speak a word against the
Son of man, it shall be forgiven him; but
whosoever shall speak against the Holy Spirit,
it shall not be forgiven him, neither in this

33 world, nor in that which is to come. Either
make the tree good, and its fruit good; or
make the tree corrupt, and its fruit corrupt:

34 for the tree is known by its fruit. Ye off-
spring of vipers, how can ye, being evil, speak
good things? for out of the abundance of the

35 heart the mouth speaketh. The good man out
of his good treasure bringeth forth good
things: and the evil man out of his evil trea-

36 sure bringeth forth evil things. And I say unto
you, that every idle word that men shall
speak, they shall give account thereof in the

37 day of judgment. For by thy words thou shalt
be justified, and by thy words thou shalt be
condemned.

A demonized man was brought to Jesus. There are
those who are ignorant of the deliverance provided in
Jesus, and some who are too incapacitated to come on
their own initiative; and these need to be brought to the
Lord by those who know the love and power of Jesus to
heal and deliver.

The Nature of Satan's Kingdom

Satan's kingdom is evil, and those who are captured by
him are placed in bondage. This wretched man's blindness and muteness were due to demonic chains. We are
not told what gave evil spirits a legal right to his life; it
could have been some curse passed down through the
transgressions of his ancestors, or because of some sin in
his own life. The church is once again beginning to recog-

nize that physical bondages are sometimes attributable to the works of the devil. It is important that the cause for men's physical infirmities be accurately diagnosed; for, if the problem is spiritual and demonic, it will never be cured by natural means.

The Nature of God's Kingdom

The power and beneficence of the Kingdom of God is reflected in the man's healing. As soon as Jesus came on the scene, the chains of infirmity were destroyed, and the afflicted was able to see and speak. So, the two kingdoms are contrasted: one puts men in bondage, and the other sets them free.

Reactions to Deliverance

Whenever deliverance takes place in public, there are a variety of reactions. Some are filled with fear and others with awe; some are believing and others unbelieving; some give praise to God and others scoff. Here we see a typical contrast of reactions. Some recognized Jesus as the Son of David, the Messiah, and others accused Him of working under the power of Beelzebub, the prince of devils.

It is a serious matter when religious leaders are blind to the working of the Holy Spirit in deliverance. They not only shut themselves off from the benefits of deliverance, but they also influence many others to reject a precious benefit of the cross. There are large segments of the church today, even some entire denominations, who are shut out from the blessings of deliverance because of the doctrinal bias of their leaders.

Ignorance Dispelled

Jesus showed how illogical these men were in attributing deliverance to the working of Beelzebub. If deliverance were of the devil, then he would be opposing himself. If a kingdom or house is divided against itself, it cannot stand; it will self-destruct. Satan is not in the business of casting out demons! He is not divided. One fact observed over and over in deliverance work is the tenacity of evil spirits to support one another. There is a unity among them that puts to shame the very body of Christ. Their unity, however, is not based on love but upon fear of authority and their propensity to evil.

Of course, Satan can and does counterfeit deliverance when it suits his purposes. There are situations where supposed "healings" take place through occult sources and white witchcraft. What appears to be a tearing down of Satan's house by his own hands is actually a deception by which he is enlarging his house. A person may be relieved of a headache and end up with cancer, for through demonic counterfeits there occurs an exchange of a lesser bondage for a greater one. The existence of the counterfeit proves the existence of the genuine. Satan could not counterfeit deliverance if no valid deliverance existed.

Deliverance Is God's Kingdom In Action

Whenever a demon is cast out, the Kingdom of God is operative. "If I by the Spirit of God cast out demons, then is the kingdom of God come upon you" (Matthew 12:28). The Kingdom of God is superior to the satanic kingdom. Satan is called "the god of this world" (II Corinthians 4:4), which means the world is under the dominion of Satan with the exception of certain people and geo-political areas which have been wrestled away from him by the army of God. The Kingdom of God is established on earth by first removing the kingdom of Satan.

The healing of the blind and dumb man involved the power of God's kingdom to overcome the devil's kingdom. This victory is won each time demons are cast out. It is not a matter of defeating isolated demons, but of confronting the whole demonic kingdom. Each demon dealt with has definite and direct connections with the kingdom he represents. There is a hierarchy of spirits which the scripture calls " principalities" and "powers...in the heavenly places" (Ephesians 6:12). Our battle is in the heavenlies; in the unseen realm of demonic activities. If we are to see the captives set free, we must learn where to battle and how.

Jesus declared that it was "by the Spirit of God" that he cast out demons, not by Beelzebub. In the parallel account (Luke 11:20) a slightly different expression is used: "If I by the finger of God cast out demons." So, "finger of God" means the same as "Spirit of God." Jesus obviously drew this expression from Exodus 8:19 where Moses and Aaron confronted Pharaoh and his magicians. When the magicians were unable to keep pace with the powers of God at work in Moses and Aaron, they confessed their inferior abilities by admitting, "This is the finger of God."

The inevitable result of the operation of God's power in the life of the believer is the defeat of the kingdom of darkness. The battle may be prolonged as we wrestle against principalities and powers, but the end result will be victory as the "finger of God" prevails.

First Bind The Strong Man

Jesus revealed how He was able to set the blind and mute man free. In doing so He revealed an important spiritual principle for us: "first bind the strong man," and then spoil his house.[23]

Wherever Satan is active, he utilizes a delegated demonic representative. This operations commander is called "the strong man." The strong man is the ruler spirit over a system of spirits. There are strong men assigned over individuals, families, churches and geo-political areas ranging from towns to nations. Jesus gave His Church power to bind the strong man and to spoil his house. This means the devil's captives are released, his control broken, his authority cancelled and his rule replaced by God's.

No Place For Neutrality

There is no middle ground in the call to spiritual warfare. Jesus clarified this truth with these words: "He that is not with me is against me" (Matthew 12:30). Those not involved in spiritual warfare and deliverance become, by

---

23 Matthew 12:29.

default, allies of Satan. Those who oppose deliverance, who say a Christian cannot have a demon, who deny the existence of demons or who label deliverance a doctrine of demons, are deceived by the devil and used by him to keep others in bondage. Some churches and entire denominations are now in this sad condition. We must pray for their eyes to be opened so that they can minister deliverance to those for whom they are responsible. They are blind to the fact that they are serving Satan.

Blaspheming the Holy Spirit

It is a serious matter to attribute the work of the Holy Spirit to Satan. Jesus said this sin would never be forgiven, either in this world or the one to come. He labeled this sin "blasphemy against the Spirit." The Pharisees were rejecting the very witness of the Spirit that was intended to bring them to saving faith.

> If I do not the works of my Father, believe me not. But if I do, though ye believe not me, believe the works: that ye may know and understand that the Father is in me, and I in the Father.
>
> John 10:37-38

Jesus declared that a tree is known by its fruit. A bad tree cannot bring forth good fruit, and a good tree cannot bring forth bad fruit. They could not label Him bad, because His fruit was good. The healing of the blind mute was good fruit. Good fruit comes from the ministry of deliverance; it is a good tree.

FILLING THE HOUSE

Matthew 12:43-45

43 But the unclean spirit, when he is gone out of
a man, passeth through waterless places,

44 seeking rest, and findeth it not. Then he
saith, I will return into my house whence I
came out; and when he is come, he findeth it

45 empty, swept, and garnished. Then goeth he,
and taketh with himself seven other spirits
more evil than himself, and they enter in and
dwell there: and the last state of that man
becometh worse than the first. Even so shall
it be also unto this evil generation.

This teaching is addressed to the scribes and Pharisees
who confronted Jesus, charging that He cast out demons
by the power of Beelzebub, the prince of demons. In the
previous section, (Matthew 12:22-42), Jesus began His
reply to His critics. Let us briefly review by outline how
Jesus responded:

1. A kingdom divided against itself cannot
   stand. Satan is not casting out demons.
2. Jesus' ministry is by the Spirit of God; and,
   whenever demons are cast out, it is evidence
   that the Kingdom of God is manifested. God's
   Kingdom has power and authority over
   Satan's kingdom.
3. Those who are not allied with Jesus in deliverance are against Him, which means they in
   actuality have sided with the devil.

4. To credit the Holy Spirit's work of deliverance to the devil is to blaspheme the Holy Spirit.
5. Since they seek a sign, the sign of the prophet Jonah will be given them: the sign of Christ's burial and resurrection. Unless they believe this sign and repent, they will be condemned.

Jesus concludes His admonition to His critics with a basic deliverance truth that they well understood.

> When a demon is cast out of a man, positive things must be brought in to replace the negative power which has been removed. Otherwise, a person will end up in worse condition than he was before his deliverance.

These religious zealots who challenged Jesus believed in taking many things out of one's life. Their doctrine was basically negative and legalistic — don't do this, and don't do that. Jesus confronts them with the necessity of a positive faith and practice. The elimination of evil things from one's life must be followed by replacement with the Person, fruit and power of the Holy Spirit, otherwise a dangerous spiritual vacuum is left.

They are faced with the claims of Christ as their Messiah. He must now fill their lives. His concluding warning to them is: unless they fill themselves with Him Who fulfills the sign of Jonah, they will be like a man delivered of demons who did not fill himself with God; "and the final condition of that man becometh worse than the first" (Matthew 12:45).

"Even so shall it be also unto this evil generation" (Matthew 12:45). The entire generation of Israelites stood in extreme spiritual peril. Unless they accepted Christ as Lord and Savior, they would end up like one freed of demons who did not thereafter fill his "house". These accusing, unbelieving religionists were headed for an irreversible judgment because of their stubborn unbelief. For "whosoever shall speak against the Holy Spirit, it shall not be forgiven him, neither in this world, nor in that which is to come" (Matthew 12:32). This is a stern warning to all who, like the scribes and Pharisees, refuse to repent of their error and continue to resist the witness of the Holy Spirit.

What about the blind and mute man who had been gloriously delivered and healed? What about the multitudes of people who had been set free from demonic bondages through the ministry of Jesus? They, too, must embrace the sign of the prophet Jonah: the death, burial and resurrection of the Son of God. Herein lay their ultimate deliverance. Unless they fill themselves with faith in Christ, their latter end will be worse than the first. The demons from which they had been freed will come back in greater force.

Living Above the Snakes

One of the things I looked forward to when our family moved to the mountains of Colorado was tromping through the forests and climbing over the rocks. But I was leery of snakes. Twice, where we lived in Texas, I had narrowly escaped snake bites while exploring rugged country. What poisonous reptiles inhabited these environs?

A native of Colorado laughed at my fears. He said, "Brother Frank, there are no poisonous snakes is these mountains. You are at ten thousand feet elevation; you live above the snakes. Snakes do not come into this altitude."

So, I lived above the snakes! This advantage represents a spiritual type. In Scripture, demons are compared with serpents and scorpions.[23] If one is being attacked by spiritual serpents (demons) he needs to climb to the safety of a greater spiritual height.

> Too, after one has had deliverance, he must purpose to climb to spiritual heights where the demons can no longer reach him.

---

23 Luke 10:19.

What are the steps to this higher height?

1. PROMPT REPENTANCE. When God discerned the evil in Cain's heart, He warned Cain in these words: "If you do well, will not your countenance be lifted up? And if you do not do well, sin is crouching at the door; and its desire is for you, but you must master it" (Genesis 4:7 NIV).

The devil, like a ferocious beast, crouched at Cain's door ready to devour him. God was calling Cain to repentance. Repentance would close the door to the enemy. Through repentance he could rule over the evil presence waiting his opportunity to strike.

This is exactly why the scripture warns each of us, "Be ye angry, and sin not: let not the sun go down upon your wrath: neither give place to the devil" (Ephesians 4:26,27). The devil is given an opportunity to attack when we neglect to repent of our anger (or any sin) before the sun goes down.

No advantage comes from postponing repentance — except the advantage given the devil to slither in. If one broods over a suffered wrong he will hatch a viper. By prompt repentance one climbs to a level where the snakes cannot reach him.

2. WALK IN LOVE. Love must direct and motivate one's life.

> Love ["God's love in us] does not insist on its own rights or its own way, for it is not self-seeking; it is not touchy or fretful or resentful; it takes no account of evil done to it — pays no attention to a suffered wrong.
>
> I Corinthians 13:5, Amplified

Most people are more aware of the wrongs done to them than they are of the wrongs they have done to others. The splinter in another's eye is more obvious than the beam in one's own eye.

For every abuse there is an abuser. It is usually the one who has been wounded who comes for counsel, not the perpetrator of the hurts. Many have come saying, "I was molested", but rarely does anyone confess, "I am a molester". Both the love that honors another and the love that forgives a trespassing brother must prevail in the life of one who expects to triumph over the devil.

Forgiveness is one of the primary ways in which love is expressed. God has set the example and standard for us by forgiving us by His love. "God commendeth his own love toward us, in that, while we were yet sinners, Christ died for us" (Romans 5:8). God's love destroyed Satan's ultimate objective. The same love-forgiveness on our part keeps us out of the devil's reach.

3. DISCIPLINED LIVING. Over and over we have discovered that undisciplined lives provide access for demon invasion. Therefore, if one expects to close the door to demons and live above the Old Serpent's fangs, he must strictly discipline every area of his life.

Undisciplined thought life can be the seed-bed for demonic infestation. When a man is born again his mind is not instantly renewed. Paul exhorted the Christians at Rome, "Be not fashioned according to this world; but be ye transformed by the renewing of your mind..." (Romans 12:2). The renewing of the mind comes through programming the mind by the Word of God. Having "this mind in you, which was also in Christ Jesus" is a daily disciplinary process.

Many Christians live defeated, discontent, depressed and discouraged lives simply because their minds are filled with garbage fed to them by the devil. One of the greatest discoveries a believer can make is that he has power over his thought life. He can choose what not to think upon and what to think upon. What is the focus of a proper thought life?

> Finally, brethren, whatsoever things are true ...honorable...just...pure...lovely...of good report; if there be any virtue, and if there be any praise, THINK ON THESE THINGS.
>
> Philippians 4:8 (Emphasis mine)

The above verse prescribes the choice of godly, edifying thoughts. If the thoughts which fill one's mind lead down a path of fear, depression, filth, unbelief and things contrary to God's Word, then one must activate his will and turn his mind-switch to "reject". Peace of mind is only a few days of self-discipline away. The choice of thoughts is ours!

The battle for the mind is a strategic battle.

Unless the battle in the mind is won, problems of the thought life will filter into the emotions and volition. For example, an unchecked thought of resentment can soon lead to feelings of bitterness and acts of retaliation. Through a lack of discipline Satan is able to build strongholds in our minds which can only be brought down by using "the weapons of our warfare...mighty before God to the casting down of strongholds" (II Corinthians 10:4).

Second, the emotions also require discipline. Most of us can readily identify with the Psalmist as he takes us on an emotional roll-a-coaster from the heights of "Oh clap your hands, all ye peoples; Shout unto God with the voice of triumph" (Psalm 47:1) to the depths of "Our soul is bowed down to the dust: Our body cleaveth unto the earth" (Psalm 44:25).

The Pslamist knew that emotional excesses were not of God because they hindered his praise and ministry to the Lord. Therefore, he dealt harshly with his soulish man: "Why are you in despair, O my soul? And why are you disturbed within me? Hope in God, for I shall again praise him, The help of my countenance, and my God" (Psalm 43:5 NAS).

Disciplined emotions are healthy emotions; channels through which we express praise, worship, love and joy.

Undisciplined emotions are channels filled with the

darkness of jealousy, hatred, anger, fear, hopelessness, self-pity and depression.

Third, the human will must be disciplined. At one end of the spectrum the will is flabby and passive, while at the opposite extreme it is rebellious and obstinate. Rebellion is a steep, downward path into the snake pit. Passivity creates a greased slide into the waiting arms of the devil. But,

> the human will that is compliant to God's will discovers fellowship with God and victory over the adversary.

"Be subject therefore to God; but resist the devil, and he will flee from you" (James 4:7).

A fourth priority of disciplined living is the bridling of the tongue.

> Every spoken word goes forth in ministry.

Our words either tear down or build up. Truly, "Death and life are in the power of the tongue" (Proverbs 18:2).

> Behold, how great a forest is set aflame by such a small fire! And the tongue is a fire, the very world of iniquity; the tongue is set among our members as that which defiles the entire body, and sets on fire the course of our life, and is set on fire by hell.
>
> James 3:5b-6 NIV

When the tongue is set on fire by hell it spews forth destructive words which serve the devil's purposes. The undisciplined tongue keeps a person kneedeep in serpents!

A fifth arena of disciplinary warfare is with the appetites of the flesh. Unrestrained lusts for food, drink and sex have brought many a person to ruin. Paul realized that his years of faithful service to God were no guarantee of continued victory. He must daily guard against disgraceful failure: "I buffet my body and make it my slave, lest possibly, after I have preached to others, I myself should be disqualified" (I Corinthians 9:27 NIV).

> The highest motivation for curbing sensual appetites and glorifying God in one's body is the continuous confession that one's body is the temple of the Holy Spirit who dwells within.[24]

4. MEET ALL TRIALS SCRIPTURALLY. None are immune from trials and testings. It is sheer unreality to think that in this life there will come a day of complete utopia. "In this world you will have trouble..." (John 16:33 NIV). The trouble with "trouble" intensifies when reactions to its pressures are wrong.

> Demon spirits find a door of entrance when life's trials are not properly resolved.

The first eight verses of the book of James are priceless. They give us God's formula for meeting trials. First, we are counseled to "Consider it pure joy...whenever you face trials of many kinds" (James 1:2 NIV). Furthermore, Jesus taught that His disciples were to "rejoice" (literal translation: exuberantly joy; leap for joy) when persecuted, reviled and falsely accused.[25] We are forced to confess that such joyful reaction to difficulties is indeed rare. Is it any marvel that the devil gains such quick advantage in times of adversity?.

The second requirement for victory in time of trial is to "let patience have its perfect work" (v.4). Some trials do

---

24 I Corinthians 6:19-20.
25 Matthew 5:11, 12.

not go away overnight; they last for days, weeks, months and years. Perseverance in faith is a mark of maturity. We display spiritual immaturity if, under testing, we lose our patience, accuse God and lash out at others.

Third, pray for wisdom. What is God saying in the midst of a trial? He is a good Heavenly Father who "gives [wisdom] generously to all without finding fault" (v.5 NIV). We must not fail to ask nor to listen for His response.

The fourth response to trials is to stand strong in faith — "believe and not doubt" (v.6 NIV). The one who wavers cannot expect anything of the Lord.

Faith is the key to receiving from God. Salvation comes by faith, the gifts of the Spirit operate by faith, healing is received through faith, God's comfort is found through faith and help in time of need comes through faith.

Double-mindedness is a curse. It keeps God's child from getting his prayers answered and causes him to be "unstable and unreliable and uncertain about everything (he thinks, feels, decides)" (James 1:8, Amplified). The double-minded man not only wears himself out but everyone else who must relate to him. For such a man there is no victory in the hour of tribulation.

6. GET YOUR FAMILY IN DIVINE ORDER. God has a special plan to protect families from the assaults of Satan. It is His blueprint for family government and is outlined in Ephesians 5:22-6:4:

(1) The husband in headship under Christ;
(2) The wife in submission to her husband as to Christ;
(3) Children in obedience and respect towards their parents in the Lord.[26]

> Households who understand, accept and adopt God's family order live above the striking power of "the old serpent, which is the Devil" Rev. 20:2.

---

26 See: Kingdom Living For the Family by Frank and Ida Mae Hammond.

Families in Divine order live in righteousness, peace and joy. Contrariwise, those who refuse and neglect God's family order invariably become vexed, beset and destroyed by the enemy.

6. BE A DOER OF THE WORD.

> The bottom line for living above the snake line is doing what God says.

A hearer only, and not a doer, deceives himself.[27] He thinks that he can get by without obeying God. He is a fool!

In the Sermon on the Mount, Jesus concluded his teaching with the parable of two builders. One built his house on a rock and the other built on sand. The time of testing came. The rain descended, the winds blew, and the floods came. These forces of nature symbolize pressures and testings that come from every direction. The house built on the rock withstood the beating, but the one built upon the sand came crashing down. What is the rock!

> Every one therefore that heareth these words of mine, and doeth them, shall be likened unto a wise man, who built his house upon the rock.
>
> Matthew 7:24.

The "rock" is hearing and doing the Word of God! A life built on anything other than obedience to the Word of God is built on sinking sand. But, isn't Jesus our Rock? Indeed! But, Jesus and His Word are inseparable.

The devil is out to destroy every life possible. If he can deceive a man into disregarding and disobeying God's Word, he can destroy that life.

There is a place in the Spirit of God where we can dwell safely. No destroyer can touch us on God's highway.

---

27 James 1:22.

> And a highway shall be there, and a way, and it shall be called *The Way of Holiness*...No lion shall be there, nor shall any ravenous beast go up thereon; they shall not be found there; but the redeemed shall walk there.
>
> Isaiah 35:8,9 (Emphasis mine)

Where do Demons Go When Cast Out?

When demons are cast out, should they be told where to go? Do we have the authority to send them to the pit, to a far country or somewhere else? Do demons just hang around the area where they are cast out unless they are specifically commanded to go to a certain destination?

There are several passages to be taken into account in answer to these questions. It should first be noted that evil spirits have great fear of their ultimate punishment when Satan and all that pertains to him will be cast into the lake of fire. (See: Revelation 20:10; 21:8). This is what some demons thought was about to happen to them when Jesus confronted them. They cried out, "Have you come to destroy us?" (Mark 1:24 NIV). In another place, the spirit identifying itself as "Legion" cried out with a loud voice, "Have you come here to torture us before the appointed time?" (Matthew 8:29 NIV). There is a certain doom awaiting demons, and that time has been determined by God. It cannot be imposed prematurely.

"Legion" also "begged Jesus again and again not to send them out of the area" (Mark 5:10 NIV). This suggests that it is possible to send evil spirits into another locale. There is no precedent in scripture for doing so; and, whether it is done or not rests on the leading of the Holy Spirit in a given situation. For a demon to be sent into a different territory would necessitate that it come under the authority of a different demonic principality and authority. For some unexplained reason evil spirits have a reluctance to change their assigned territories.

Finally, "the demons begged Jesus, 'Send us among the pigs; allow us to go into them.' He gave them permission, and the evil spirits came out and went into the pigs" (Mark 5:12-13 NIV). Again, no explanation is given as to why Jesus gave this permission. The incident reveals:

(1) That Jesus considered the welfare of men above that of animals;

(2) That evil spirits can and do indwell animals;

(3) That if a demon cannot indwell a person it prefers an animal over being sent out of the area;

(4) That the goal of indwelling spirits is destruction;

(5) That spirits cast out of people can be given permission to enter into animals.

Since Jesus did not follow this procedure of sending demons into animals in any other recorded deliverance, it seems unwise for us to make it a matter of routine practice. We are often prone to look for fixed methods instead of learning to follow the voice of the Holy Spirit. What does He tell us to do? Where there is a clear instruction in the Word of God it is obvious what we must do. The Holy Spirit will never lead anyone to do anything contrary to the Word of God. At times, when several scriptural alternatives are available, we must receive our specific direction from the Holy Spirit.

There is one instance when Jesus forbade a spirit to return to a person once it was cast out. "He rebuked the evil spirit. 'You deaf and mute spirit,' he said, 'I command you, come out of him and never enter him again'" (Mark 9:25 NIV). This was the case of a demonized child whose father was responsible for the child's spiritual protection. Since the father did not give a clear declaration of faith, Jesus sovereignly provided for the child's protection from the return of the tormenting and destructive spirit by forbidding it to return to the child.

If it were intended that in every situation demons be bound from returning, then Jesus would not have taught that they could return and would, indeed, attempt to do so. Maintaining deliverance is not based upon sending demons to a far country!

Protection against demons returning is in becoming filled with the things of God.

Jesus said that when a demon goes out of a man, it wanders in dry places. It does not hang around; but, if it finds no relief elsewhere, it will soon return to inspect the place from which it was driven. If the "house" (life of the person) is left empty, the demon will reenter and may bring other spirits with him — even some more wicked than himself!

There is much more involved in being free than having demons cast out. Once demons are cast out, a person must fill himself with the opposite of that from which he was delivered. Others may encourage and help the delivered person to stay free, but it becomes the personal responsibility of that individual to fill his own house.

Do Demons Leave A Person On Their Own Volition?

The phrase, "when he is gone out" in Matthew 12:43, has been interpreted by some to mean that demons sometimes leave a person of their own volition. This is mere conjecture. The context of the passage begins with Jesus forcing a demon to leave by casting him out. Joseph Henry Thayer, a widely recognized Greek authority, say the phrase "is gone out" speaks "of those expelled or cast out (esp. of demons driven forth from a body of which they have held possession."[28] Thus, the spirit is gone out as a result of having been cast out; he has not left of his own volition.

Notice, too, that the "going out" of a demon presupposes its having been inside a person. Some people are needlessly embarrassed to admit that evil spirits are within them. This has resulted in the adoption of evasive terminology. For example, instead of admitting demonization a person may say that he is oppressed.

---

28 Thayer, Greek-English Lexicon of the New Testament, P. 222.

> Deliverance is not a matter of brushing demons off the shoulders; it is casting them out!

"My House"

When demons speak through persons during the process of deliverance, they often refer to the indwelt person's body as "my house." If that person is a Christian, then the claim of ownership is unfounded. The believer has been purchased by the blood of Jesus and belongs to the Lord. This claim of ownership is a deceptive ploy of demons to try to make a deliverance minister think that the demon has a legal right to that person and, therefore, give up his attack against him.

Worse Than The First

It is clear from Jesus' reference to "more wicked" spirits that demons vary in degrees of wickedness. All of them are evil, but some are more vile than others.

Demons also possess varying degrees of strength. This is indicated in the case of the epileptic, when Jesus said, "This kind goeth not out save by prayer and fasting" (Matthew 17:21, Margin).

How serious is the possibility of spirits returning in greater force than when they left? Since evil spirits can do no more than they are permitted to do, the answer to this question is relevant to the spiritual commitment of the person receiving deliverance. Therefore, those who minister deliverance should be prudent as to whom they minister. For example, how could an unbeliever be expected to stay free and prevent greater demonization from occurring? With what would he possibly fill himself? Unless he gave his heart and life to Jesus immediately and began to fill himself with active truth, he would be absolutely vulnerable.

Occasionally, a believer expresses fear of deliverance because he remembers the scripture warning that demons can return in greater number and force. However, this is very rare. The reason it is rare is because most Christians, after deliverance, go forward in the ways of the Lord. From actual experience we have seen VERY FEW cases where the latter state of a person was worse than before. Some lose what they gained, but few lose more than they gain.

A wise minister will teach the newly set free the importance of filling their houses.

> There is no lasting benefit from having demons cast out unless they are kept out.

The ideal candidate for deliverance is one whose motive is growth in Christlikeness rather than relief from problems.

PARABLE OF THE SOWER

Mark 4:3,4,15; Matthew 13:3,4,18-19; Luke 8:5,6,12

3,4 Hearken: Behold, the sower went forth to
sow: and it came to pass, as he sowed, some
seed fell by the way side, and the birds came
and devoured it...

15 And these are they by the way side, where the
word is sown; and when they have heard,
straightway cometh Satan, and taketh away
the word which hath been sown in them.

The seed, the gospel of the Kingdom, falls on different
types of soil, which represent the hearts of hearers.

Satan is a thief. He knows the potential growth of the
truth received by faith into men's hearts. And Satan
knows that truth sets men free.[29] Unless the Word is
mixed with faith by him who hears it, then that truth will
not penetrate into his heart, but will remain on the sur-
face of his consciousness, and Satan, like an evil bird, will
snatch it away.

This explains why some who are exposed to truth never
develop spiritually. It takes a heart of faith to receive God's
Word.[30] Unless the Word is believed and acted upon, it is
soon snatched away by the devil and is forgotten.

Also, the seed that fell among thorns is choked to death
by the "cares of the world, and the deceitfulness of riches"
(Mark 4:18). Forget not that Satan is "the god of this

---

29 John 8:32.
30 Hebrews 4:2.

world" (II Corinthians 4:4); therefore, worldly influences are directly of the devil. A Christian who is conformed to this world is like a field filled with tares. No matter how much seed of truth is sown into his heart it is soon choked out, and there is no lasting benefit. A man must give up the world to receive Christ. As a Christian he must continue to give up the world in order to grow spiritually.

PARABLE OF TARES

Matthew 13:24,25,37-39

24 The kingdom of heaven is likened unto a man
25 that sowed good seed in his field: but while men slept, his enemy came and sowed tares
26 also among the wheat, and went away. But when the blade sprang up, and brought forth
37 fruit, then appeared the tares also... He that
38 soweth the good seed is the Son of man; and the field is the world; and the good seed, these are the sons of the kingdom; and the
39 tares are the sons of the evil one; and the enemy that sowed them is the devil: and the harvest is the end of the world; and the reapers are angels.

Jesus is the One who sowed the good seed in the world. He planted His children and His Church in the world. Then Satan came under the cover of darkness, when men were spiritually asleep, and sowed his children in the earth. Good and evil will develop side by side until the time of the final judgment. Then there will be a time of separation when the righteous who belong to Christ will be gathered unto Him, and those who belong to the devil will be burned with fire.

Thus, this parable reveals the root cause underlying the wickedness found in the world and why God has not already judged it. In light of this revelation we should be more determined than ever to stand true to Jesus Christ and His gospel. Let the true sons of God shine brighter and brighter amid the demonic darkness, for the time of judgment draws near.

THE GADARENE DEMONIAC

Mark 5:1-20; Matthew 8:28-34; **Luke 8:26-39**

26 And they arrived at the country of the

27 Gerasenes, which is over against Galilee. And when he was come forth upon the land, there met him a certain man out of the city, who had demons; and for a long time he had worn no clothes, and abode not in any house, but

28 in the tombs. And when he saw Jesus, he cried out, and fell down before him, and with a loud voice said, What have I to do with thee, Jesus, thou Son of the Most High God? I

29 beseech thee, torment me not. For he was commanding the unclean spirit to come out from the man. For often-times it had seized him: and he was kept under guard, and bound with chains and fetters; and breaking the bands asunder, he was driven of the demon

30 into the deserts. And Jesus asked him, What is thy name? And he said, Legion; for many

31 demons were entered into him. And they intreated him that he would not command

32 them to depart into the abyss. Now there was there a herd of many swine feeding on the mountain: and they intreated him that he would give them leave to enter into them. And

33 he gave them leave. And the demons came out from the man, and entered into the swine:

and the herd rushed down the steep into the
34 lake, and were drowned. And when they that
fed them saw what had come to pass, they
fled, and told it in the city and in the country.
35 And they went out to see what had come to
pass; and they came to Jesus, and found the
man, from whom the demons were gone out,
sitting, clothed and in his right mind, at the
36 feet of Jesus: and they were afraid. And they
that saw it told them how he that was pos-
37 sessed with demons was made whole. And all
the people of the country of the Gerasenes
round about asked him to depart from them;
for they were holden with great fear: and he
38 entered into a boat, and returned. But the
man from whom the demons were gone out
prayed him that he might be with him: but he
39 sent him away, saying, Return to thy house,
and declare how great things God hath done
for thee. And he went his way, publishing
throughout the whole city how great things
Jesus had done for him.

The Highly Demonized

Today, mental health professionals diagnose persons
like this Gadarene as being mentally ill. They are institu-
tionalized and tranquilized.

> Judging from both scriptural evidence and
> practical experience it can be assumed that many
> who are confined in mental institutions could be
> healed through deliverance.

Telltale evidences of demonization seen here include:
1. Preoccupation with death: The Gadarene
    dwelt among the tombs.
2. Supernatural strength: he could not be
    restrained with chains.

3. Ferociousness: he was like a wild animal. No man had been able to tame him.
4. Destructive and injurious: he cut himself with stones and was suicidal.
5. Schizophrenic characteristics: a divided personality.
   (1) Something in him wanted to worship Jesus.
   (2) Something in him wanted nothing to do with Jesus.
6. Something in him felt threatened by the presence of Jesus and pleaded not to be tormented.

What Jesus Did

1. Jesus commanded the demon to come out. He was in complete command of the situation. He knew what He was doing. The verb "was commanding" (Luke 8:29) expresses continuous action. Jesus was pressuring or wrestling the unclean spirit by the repeated commands to come out.
2. He required the demon to identify himself. Jesus was certainly not ignorant of the demon's identity, and neither was information from a demonic source necessary to accomplish the deliverance. When this strong spirit was forced to name himself, his power was weakened, as is evidenced by the demon's pleading with Jesus not to send them into the abyss.
3. He cast the demons out with His authority.
4. He granted Legion permission to enter the swine.[31]

Which of the following reasons seems most plausible as to why Jesus permitted the demons to enter the swine?
   (1) Jesus hated pigs.
   (2) Jesus wanted to teach the pig farmers a lesson.
   (3) Jesus was sympathetic toward demons.

---

31 Luke 8:31,32.

(4) Jesus wanted to avoid further confrontation.
(5) Jesus wanted to spare the demoniac from being torn by so many spirits, and granting them permission to enter the swine caused them to leave without resistance.[32]

Additional Insights Into Demons

1. One person can be indwelt by thousands of spirits. A legion would represent as many as five thousand.
2. Indwelling demons work together as a rank of soldiers under a single commander. Satan's kingdom is not divided in its evil work.
3. Demons are fearful of the torment awaiting them in their time of final judgment.

Repercussions And Results From Deliverance

1. The swine feeders "fled" in fear and alarmed the whole city.
2. The townspeople were upset over the material loss of the swine and "holden with great fear" over the strange explanation given. They intreated Jesus to depart from their borders.
3. The demoniac was blessed and became a disciple. He wanted to remain with Jesus permanently.
4. The friends of the former demoniac and those who heard his testimony "marvelled" (Mark 5:20).

---

32 The author holds to this view.

ANOTHER DELIVERANCE HEALING AND BLASPHEMOUS ACCUSATION

Matthew 9:32-34

32 And as they went forth, behold, there was brought to him a dumb man possessed with

33 a demon. And when the demon was cast out the dumb man spake: and the multitudes marvelled, saying, It was never so seen in

34 Israel. But the Pharisees said, By the prince of demons casteth he out demons.

The Value of Testimonies

There were multitudes responding to the ministry of Jesus due to the testimony of those who had been healed and delivered. In this context two men healed of blindness "went forth, and spread abroad his fame in all the land;" and, among those who came to Jesus, was this man under the power of a dumb spirit. When the demon was cast out, the man could speak.

Jesus And His Deliverance Ministry Judged To Be Of Satan

The Pharisees again charged that Jesus was of the devil and performing these miracles by Satanic power. Undoubtedly the Pharisees were concerned over the ministry of Jesus, for the people were responding to Him en masse. What Jesus was doing was so divergent from their own practices that they were unable to tolerate Him, and what He taught was so authoritative that they were unable to refute Him. They faced the same decision which every person faces concerning the identity of Jesus. Jesus must either be accepted for who He says He is, or rejected as false. In making this decision men must be sure that they are not influenced within themselves by pride, jealousy or religious prejudice.

It is sobering to realize that religious men who spent their lives studying the prophecies of the coming Messiah were unable to recognize Him and accept Him when He came. Deception and error are subtle enemies seeking to ensnare all who profess to follow God. Paul reminded Timothy that men who are full of pride and unteachable are vulnerable to falling into the same condemnation into which the devil himself once fell.[33] Let every seeker of truth have a teachable spirit and pray daily for deliverance from the deceptive snares of the devil.

---

33 I Timothy 3:6.

THE TWELVE COMMISSIONED AND ANOINTED

Mark 6:7; **Matthew 10:1,5-8;** Luke 9:1-2

1   And he called unto him his twelve disciples,
    and gave them authority over unclean spirits
    to cast them out, and to heal all manner of

5   disease and all manner of sickness. These
    twelve Jesus sent forth, and charged them
    saying, Go not into any way of the Gentiles,
    and enter not into any city of the Samaritans:

6   but go rather to the lost sheep of the house of

7   Israel. And as ye go, preach, saying, The king-

8   dom of heaven is at hand. Heal the sick, raise
    the dead, cleanse the lepers, cast out
    demons: freely ye received, freely give.

Calling And Equipping

There are callings of God within callings. Jesus had called these twelve men to be apostles, and now he called them into specialized ministries. The servants of the Lord must always remain open to what their Master calls them to do. We are taught not to compare ourselves and our ministries to others but to be faithfully obedient to our Master's instructions. The Lord has called some today to special ministries of healing and deliverance.

God called me to the ministry at age twenty six. He called me to the ministry of deliverance at age forty-seven. Jesus stood at the head of my bed one night and called,

89

"Frank, Frank!" He awakened my wife as a witness to the call. Without waking up in the natural, I answered Him out of my spirit, "Jesus? Jesus!" He said, "I have called you by name". What could another calling be? Immediately we were thrust into the ministry of deliverance. We never sought this ministry. Rather, people began to seek us out from far and wide requesting deliverance. The gifts of the Holy Spirit began to flow — discerning of spirits, words of knowledge and faith.

Whomever the Lord calls, He equips. Since these men were to cast out demons, He "gave them authority over unclean spirits". Moses did not feel that he was equipped when God called him at the burning bush and commissioned him to be a deliverer of God's people; but, as Moses went forth in obedience, the equipping was evident. This pattern of God's equipping of the called is consistent throughout scripture. When Jesus commissioned the twelve, the seventy, and the Church, He gave them authority and power.

> And he called the twelve together, and gave them POWER and AUTHORITY over all demons, and to cure diseases.
>
> Luke 9:1 (Emphasis mine)

"Power" and "authority" represent separate but compatible facets of equipping for ministry.

"Authority" (Greek: *exousia*) is the ability and strength with which one is endued. In the hands of men, it is an extension of the Lord's authority, for Jesus declared that ALL authority was given to Him in heaven and on earth.[34]

Authority to cast out demons has been given to all believers: "...in my name they shall cast out demons" (Mark 16:17). This divinely bestowed authority is available to every Christian who has the faith to appropriate it. The

---

34 Matthew 28:18.

devil is delighted when Christ's disciples allow their authority to lie dormant.

"Power" (Greek: *dunamis*) is power in action; it is the power that brings forth miracles; it is the power of the Holy Spirit. Just before His ascension Jesus promised, "But ye shall receive power, when the Holy Spirit is come upon you" (Acts 1:8). This promise was initially fulfilled at Pentecost when the one hundred and twenty disciples were all filled with the Holy Spirit.[35] The good news is that "For to you is the promise, and to your children, and to all that are afar off, even as many as the Lord our God shall call unto him" (Acts 2:29).

The power given to believers is channeled through the gifts of the Holy Spirit which include gifts of healing, miracles and discerning of spirits. An example of a miraculous healing and deliverance is found in Acts 19:11,12:

> And God wrought special miracles by the hands of Paul; insomuch that unto the sick were carried away from his body handkerchiefs or aprons, and the diseases departed from them, and the evil spirits went out.

The power of the Holy Spirit in operation through a believer is commonly identified as "the anointing". Anyone who has ever functioned under the anointing of the Holy spirit knows that the anointing is not constant — it is greater at some times than at others. Authority is constant, but power can be enhanced. Prayer and fasting are spiritual disciplines which increase the anointing.

When the disciples failed to drive out certain demons Jesus instructed them, "This kind can come out by nothing, save by prayer and fasting" (Mark 9:29).[36]. "This kind" could only be driven out with anointing. The spiritual discipline of prayer and fasting would increase their power.

Sometimes we ponder why we do not enjoy the same degree of anointing with which Jesus healed and delivered. This is the same question the twelve asked of Jesus, "How is it that we could not cast it out?" (Mark 9:28). As

---

35 Acts 2:4.
36 Many ancient authorities add "and fasting".

with them, our potential is contingent upon commitment and discipline.

The power and authority to cast out ALL demons has been given to the Church. We have power to dispossess them and cast them out — no matter how many, how crafty, how hellish or how obstinate. Therefore, every failure and partial success must be chalked up to our own shortcoming.

Those who go forth in obedience and faith will experience the anointing of the Holy Spirit. The gospel will be confirmed with signs following.[37]

Limitations On Ministry

The Lord set limitations on the ministry of the twelve. They were not at this time to go to Gentiles or Samaritans. God has a timing in what He does, and a big part of cooperating with God's will is in working within the limitations He establishes.

Deliverance is not to be ministered indiscriminately. The Lord will send us to the ones to whom He would have us go.

Healing And Deliverance

Healing and deliverance are companion ministries. Deliverance often results in physical healing and even more often in emotional healing.

> Physical healing is often the byproduct of a thorough deliverance.

For example, persons in bondage to resentment, hatred and unforgivingness are often victims of headaches, stomach disorders, arthritis and tumors. When forgiveness and reconciliation are established, and the evil spirits associated with the root of bitterness are cast out, then healing is often manifested.

---

37 Mark 16:14-20.

Freely Give

Jesus instructed these men to freely give what they had freely received. They could freely give truth, healing and deliverance to others, for they were the recipients of these blessings. They had nothing except that which they had received from their Master. They were to go forth with a giving attitude, not thinking of what they might gain for their work.

The Jewish exorcists no doubt were accustomed to require pay, just as physicians received pay for healing the sick. The twelve could easily have obtained large sums of money for the miracles which they were empowered to perform. They, however, must not seek personal gain nor be anxious about their livelihood.

Simon Magnus sought to purchase the power of the Holy Spirit.[38] It is not for sale; it is freely given of the Lord. It is not obtained by expensive pursuits of education and labor.

> The anointing is received as a gift, and the Lord expects it to be administered in the same spirit of grace.

The twelve were working for the Lord, and He was responsible for them. As they gave, it would be given unto them; for He would cause men to put into their bosoms good measure, pressed down, heaped up and running over.

Avarice and the love of money has caused many ministers to fall into the snare of the devil. The trend today is to commercialize the gospel. Too many today see the preaching of the gospel as a profession for money-making rather than as a ministry. God's servants are exhorted to tend the flock of God, "not motivated by the advantages and profits [belonging to the office] but eagerly and cheerfully" (I Peter 5:2, Amplified).

---

38 Acts 8:18.

Instructions and Exhortations

In the immediate context which we have been following in Matthew 10, guidelines were given to the twelve as to how they were to conduct themselves. These instructions provide practical direction for today's traveling ministers.

The disciples were instructed how to conduct themselves in the homes where they lodged. They were grounded in what course of action to follow when accepted and when not accepted.

They could expect to encounter danger from time to time, so they were counseled to be as wise as serpents and as harmless as doves. They must beware of men and not invite trouble by foolish actions. When they were brought before religious and civil authorities, they should consider such confrontations God-ordained opportunities to represent Him. The Holy Spirit would give them wisdom in such times, so they need not premeditate what they would say.

So, today, Jesus is teaching that ones who are in the will of God can still run into difficulties. We must not panic or blame the devil but trust in God's providence.

Since they called the Master of the house Beelzebub, His disciples cannot anticipate better treatment. Intimidation and persecution is to be anticipated. Why are not all church leaders obedient to the Lord's commission to cast out demons? Sometimes it is because of ignorance but more often it is because of fear. How will the people react? What will my peers think? What will my denominational leaders do?

The fear of man has caused some to refuse or abandon the commission to deliverance.

PERSECUTION
ENCOUNTERED

Matthew 10:24-27

24 A disciple is not above his teacher, nor a servant
25 above his lord. It is enough for the disciple
that he be as his teacher, and the servant as
his lord. If they have called the master of the
house Beelzebub, how much more them of
26 his household! Fear them not therefore: for
there is nothing covered, that shall not be
revealed; and hid, that shall not be known.
27 What I tell you in the darkness, speak ye in
the light; and what ye hear in the ear, proclaim upon the housetops.

Even though Jesus went about doing good and healing
all that were oppressed of the devil,[39] He was not always
welcomed and appreciated. After He delivered the
Gadarene demoniac from oppressing spirits, the people
asked Him to leave their community. On several occasions
the Pharisees called Him Beelzebub and accused Him of
casting out demons by the power of the devil.

Now, Jesus tells his disciples that they can expect similar treatment, for the disciple is not above his Master.
Today's deliverance ministers are no exception. Wherever
and whenever demons are cast out there will be objections
and criticisms — always from the religious community.

---

39 Acts 10:38.

> In spite of the positive results of deliverance, the minister often finds himself ridiculed and his ministry resisted.

It is paradoxical that those who attack the ministers and ministry of deliverance are acting under the devil's influence. In fact most of those who are outspoken against deliverance are secretly harboring evil in their lives. Hypocrites fear exposure.

The deliverance minister's responsibility in the Lord is to be a faithful steward of the truth entrusted to him. Let God's saints faithfully reveal His truths, and He will in due course confirm their integrity.

Fear Not

When persecution is experienced, the disciple must not yield to fear. Three times in this context Jesus tells His disciples not to be afraid. To strengthen them against the temptation to fear, He teaches them several spiritual principles:

1. Disciples should anticipate opposition and persecution. There is a price to pay for being a follower of Jesus.
2. Everything covered and hid shall eventually be brought to light. The teaching He has given them is truth. Even though they have received it privately, it must be shouted from the housetops. Evil and error are to be judged and defeated by the light of truth.
3. Fear is the enemy of boldness. Fear of man will rob Christ's servants of their boldness to proclaim His truth.
4. Faithfulness to God is more important than life itself. It is better to die than to deny. Therefore, reverential fear of God must replace one's cringing fear of man.
5. The disciple's reward is with God. He knows each hair of our heads, and He knows the

condition of each little sparrow. We are valuable in the sight of God. If we should die for His sake, our deaths will not go unnoticed or unrewarded.

6. Truth divides. There are always some who are unteachable. Divisions are necessary in order that those who are genuine will be manifested.

No doubt there have to be differences among you to show which of you have God's approval.

I Corinthians 11:19.

DELIVERANCE IS THE CHILDREN'S BREAD

Mark 7:24-30; Matthew 15:21-28

24 And from thence he arose, and went away into the borders of Tyre and Sidon. And he entered into a house, and would have no man

25 know it; and he could not be hid. But straightway a woman, whose little daughter had an unclean spirit, having heard of him,

26 came and fell down at his feet. Now the woman was a Greek, a Syrophonecian by race. And she besought him that he would

27 cast forth the demon out of her daughter. And he said unto her, Let the children first be filled: for it is not meet to take the children's

28 bread and cast it to the dogs. But she answered and saith unto him, Yea, Lord; even the dogs under the table eat of the children's

29 crumbs. And he said unto her, For this saying go thy way; the demon is gone out of thy daughter.

30 And she went away unto her house, and found the child laid upon the bed, and the demon gone out.

Principles of Deliverance

The above passage is a valuable source of spiritual principles pertaining to deliverance:

1. Children can be demonized. The diminutive form for "daughter" is employed in the Greek, and this signifies a very young daughter.

2. Parents are the spiritual custodians and guardians of their young children. Children are unable to protect themselves or initiate their own petitions for deliverance. Parents should seek Christ's ministry for their children. It is especially the responsibility of fathers,[40] as God-ordained heads of families.[41] This text makes no mention of the child's father; perhaps he was deceased, or not in agreement with the his wife's search for spiritual answers and solutions. In the absence of a father's headship, the mother acts on behalf of her children.

3. Deliverance is "the children's bread." That is, deliverance is for God's people. The passage makes the point that this woman was a Greek by birth and a Syrophonecian by nationality. She was not an Israelite and therefore not of God's people through descendants from Abraham; Jesus, therefore, initially ignored the woman's plea for her daughter's deliverance. As the woman persisted, Jesus recognized her faith, which qualified her as a true spiritual daughter of Abraham, for Abraham himself was accounted righteous by faith.[42] When faith was exhibited, the daughter received deliverance.

4. Persons can be delivered from demons without being in the presence of the deliverance minister. The little girl was not with her mother but at home. Jesus cast out the spirits from a distance. There is no problem of time or distance when addressing the spirit realm.

---

40 Ephesians 6:4.
41 Ephesians 5:23; I Timothy 3:4, 12.
42 Genesis 15:6.

Note: The practice of deliverance at a distance should be kept within the concept represented by the parent-child relationship. The criteria for such ministry rests upon the persons' dependancy on a spiritual covering rather than upon his inability to be present.

Should someone desire ministry who is unable to be present, an anointed item could be taken to him.[43] Once again, let it be emphasized that the guidance of the Holy Spirit is needed.

5. Faith is important to deliverance: "O woman, great is thy faith; be it done unto thee even as thou wilt" (Matthew 15:28). The blessings of God are reserved for those who believe.[44] Deliverance is no exception. Faith is required for salvation, the baptism in the Holy Spirit, healing, deliverance and all that one receives from God. Someone may receive deliverance on the faith of another, but he must retain it by his own faith. The Bible teaching and counseling which accompanies deliverance (whether public or private) serves the purpose of building faith in the one seeking deliverance. Bringing one to a position of faith is an essential part of effective ministry.

Note: The Syrophonecian woman was not an unbeliever seeking deliverance. She called Jesus "Lord" and asked for a blessing from her "Master's" table. Her whole demeanor exhibited her faith, which Jesus immediately recognized and rewarded.

---

43 Acts 19:11, 12.
44 Hebrews 11:6.

BINDING AND LOOSING

Matthew 16:13-19; Mark 8:27-30; Luke 9:18-21

13 Now when Jesus came into the parts of Caesarea Philippi, he asked his disciples, saying, Who do men say that the Son of man is?

14 And they said, Some say John the Baptist; some, Elijah; and others Jeremiah, or one of

15 the prophets. He saith unto them, But who say

16 ye that I am? And Simon Peter answered and said, Thou art the Christ, the Son of the living

17 God. And Jesus answered and said unto him, Blessed art thou, Simon Bar-Jonah: for flesh and blood hath not revealed it unto thee, but

18 my Father who is in heaven. And I also say unto thee, that thou art Peter, and upon this rock I will build my church; and the gates of

19 Hades shall not prevail against it. I will give unto thee the keys of the kingdom of heaven: and whatsoever thou shalt bind on earth shall be bound in heaven; and whatsoever thou shalt loose on earth shall be loosed in heaven.

Basis For The Believer's Authority

Jesus raised the question as to His true identity. Do men know who He is? Most saw Him as one of the prophets returned from the dead. They saw Him as someone special but not as God's Son.

Whom do the chosen twelve see Him to be? Peter, as the spokesman, responds, "Thou art the Christ, the Son of the living God." Jesus congratulates Peter on His spiritual insight. Peter had truly received a revelation from the Heavenly Father.

Jesus asked this question for a reason. What He was about to teach them required that they first know unequivocally who He is. HIS NAME IS SYNONYMOUS WITH HIS AUTHORITY. They must know this truth in order to understand His Church and its mission of spiritual warfare. His Church is built upon the rock (foundation) of His name (authority). The gates of Hades shall not prevail against the Church. That is, His Church will be a militant church: an army. It will go forth in His name and carry the battle against "the gates of Hades (the powers of the infernal region)" (Amplified Bible), and those gates will fall.

The Church And Spiritual Warfare

1. Jesus builds His Church.
2. In order to be effective in spiritual warfare His disciples must recognize the authority, represented in His name, upon which His Church is built.
3. His Church is called to aggressive spiritual warfare.
4. The gates of the Satanic kingdom, whose intent is death and destruction, shall not withstand the Church's assault.
5. Jesus has provided His Church with the keys of the Kingdom of Heaven by which His Church will accomplish its victory.
6. These keys are the power to bind and loose. Keys are the symbols of authority. For example, if you have the keys to an automobile, you can loose it by unlocking the door, starting the engine and driving away. Or you use your key to bind the automobile by shutting off the engine and locking the doors. Thus, the church is given authority to control the activities of the evil principalities and powers in the heavens.

7. These keys do not, as sometimes interpreted, represent authority to enter the Kingdom of Heaven but rather the ability to function in Kingdom authority. They are keys "of" the Kingdom rather than keys "to" the Kingdom.

8. The "gates of Hades" represent the government of the Satanic kingdom. In the Old Testament the gates of a city represented its place of authority. The king and the elders of a city would meet in the gates to transact official business. Here the decisions and strategies of war were devised.

9. To overthrow the gates means to take the offensive against the enemy and defeat him while he is yet making his plot against you. This is what Jesus declared His Church would do. The Church is now taking offensive action and through spiritual warfare attacking the gates of Hades.

10. What is bound or loosed on earth must first be bound or loosed in the heavens. The verbs "shall be bound" and "shall be loosed" are perfect, passive participles. This indicates that whatever is bound or loosed on earth is that which is already in a state of having been bound or loosed in the heavens. This binding and loosing in the heavens represents the Church's exercise of its authority over the Satanic realm as it wrestles against the principalities and powers in the heavens.[45]

---

45 For a fuller treatment, See: *The Saints At War* by Frank Hammond, Chapter IV.

MEN USED OF GOD ARE SOMETIMES USED OF SATAN

Matthew 16:21-23

21 From that time began Jesus to shew unto his
   disciples, that he must go unto Jerusalem,
   and suffer many things of the elders and chief
   priests and scribes, and be killed, and the

22 third day be raised up. And Peter took him,
   and began to rebuke him, saying, Be it far
   from thee, Lord: this shall never be unto thee.

23 But he turned, and said unto Peter, Get thee
   behind me, Satan: thou art a stumbling-block
   unto me: for thou mindest not the things of
   God, but the things of men.

Men Are Fallible

There is mixture in man. The same Peter who moments
earlier spoke by divine revelation then became the mouth-
piece of Satan!

We must recognize that every man is fallible. It is dangerous to elevate any man, however much he has been
used of God and however much truth he has proclaimed,
and make that man one's infallible "Pope."

Many leaders have become "popes" in the eyes of their
followers. When they teach false doctrine, the whole following goes over the cliff together. Some ministers promote and encourage such blind commitment to them-

selves and see themselves as infallible. For example, they might see themselves as modern-day apostles and reason that since apostles were used to write most of the New Testament, and therefore were infallible in what they wrote, it follows that as today's apostles they are infallible. Such self-aggrandizement is sheer deception and self-delusion. "Let him that thinketh he standeth, take heed lest he fall" (I Corinthians 7:37).

In other instances, leaders are made to be "popes" by their constituents. Some disciples will listen to the voice of only one minister. Paul warned against such limitations, and labeled those who practiced such exclusiveness as "yet carnal" and engenderers of envying, strife and division.[46]

There is a balance and safety in hearing the teachings of all of God's messengers. Not any one minister has full insight into the things of God. "Therefore, let no man glory in men. For all things are yours; whether Paul, or Apollos, or Cephas...all are yours" (I Corinthians 3:22).

The Bible is the criteria for judging every man's message. Jesus was showing His disciples (undoubtedly from the Old Testament prophecies) how He must go to Jerusalem, suffer, die, and be raised the third day.[47] When Peter rebuked Jesus for saying that He must die, Peter was speaking contrary to the Word of God. His opinion was pure error. He had become Satan's instrument. Jesus rebuked Peter as Satan!

Jesus Is Worthy

Jesus alone is worthy to be the Head of His church. All men, however exalted by self or others, have feet of clay. Many men who have been mighty spokesmen for God have later fallen into Satan's traps and become his pawns. King Saul was such a man. He was chosen and anointed as King. He prophesied by the Spirit of God. Then, through his disobedience and rebellion, he lost his anointing and became troubled and controlled by an evil spirit.[48]

---

46 I Corinthians 3:1-4.
47 Matthew 16:21.
48 I Samuel 15-16.

A DELIVERANCE FAILURE

Matthew 17:14-21; **Mark 9:14-29;** Luke 9:37-43

14 And when they came to the disciples, they saw a great multitude about them, and

15 scribes questioning with them. And straightway all the multitude, when they saw him, were greatly amazed, and running to him

16 saluted him. And he asked them, What ques-

17 tion ye with them? And one of the multitude answered him, Teacher, I brought unto thee

18 my son, who hath a dumb spirit; and wheresoever it taketh him, it dasheth him down: and he foameth, and grindeth his teeth, and pineth away: and I spake to thy disciples that they should cast it out; and they were not

19 able. And he answereth them and saith, O faithless generation, how long shall I be with you? how long shall I bear with you? bring

20 him unto me. And they brought him unto him: and when he saw him, straightway the spirit tare him grievously; and he fell on the

21 ground, and wallowed foaming. And he asked his father, How long time is it since this hath come upon him? And he said, From a child.

22 And oft-times it hath cast him both into the fire and into the waters, to destroy him: but if

thou canst do anything, have compassion on

23 us, and help us. And Jesus said unto him, If thou canst! All things are possible to him that

24 believeth. Straightway the father of the child cried out, and said, I believe; help thou mine

25 unbelief. And when Jesus saw that a multitude came running together, he rebuked the unclean spirit, saying unto him, Thou dumb and deaf spirit, I command thee, come out of

26 him, and enter no more into him. And having cried out, and torn him much, he came out: and the boy became as one dead; insomuch

27 that the more part said, He is dead. But Jesus took him by the hand, and raised him

28 up; and he arose. And when he was come into the house, his disciples asked him privately,

29 How is it that we could not cast it out? And he said unto them, This kind can come out by nothing, save by prayer. (See Margin: Many ancient authorities add "and fasting").

A Concerned Father

A certain man beseeched Jesus for the deliverance of his son who was dumb and sore vexed. The boy's seizures caused him often to fall into fire and water.

Seizures can be purely demonic, although some are found to be the result of brain damage. The devil's intentions to kill his victims is clearly evidenced. Satan would cause this boy to be burned to death or drowned. "The thief cometh not, but for to steal, and to kill, and to destroy" (John 10:10a).

The Disciples Fail

The disciples had attempted this boy's deliverance but had failed. It grieves the heart of Jesus when we fail in ministry. Listen to Jesus's lament: "O faithless and perverse generation, how long shall I bear with you?" (Matthew 17:17).

Why They Failed

Jesus had called, commissioned, and endued these disciples with authority to cast out ALL demons.[49] How could they have failed? How could we fail? Jesus put his finger on the problem. They were "faithless." This word means: unsteadfast, unfaithful, untrustworthy, unbelieving. Furthermore, they were "perverse." This word literally means: turned aside; corrupted. In other words, the disciples had not come into a full maturity of faith and commitment.

Learning From Our Failures

However, the disciples were genuinely concerned over their failure. They had experienced great successes in casting out demons. They were teachable and open to correction. What minister has not faced a similar dilemma? We must remain humble and teachable. When we fail, we must also go to Jesus and ask His assessment.

Each person's need for deliverance is important. We must seek to be at our best, for we are dealing with the lives of persons for whom Christ died. Who can claim to be as effective as Jesus? Yet we must not be satisfied with partial success, but press on in Him unto full ability.

Demonic problems are "mountains" in the lives of those who have them. Jesus taught that faith the size of a mustard seed is enough to remove mountains.[50]

> Casting out demons is a mountain-removal ministry requiring faith.

As Christians we should cultivate faith and maintain it, for there will continually be opportunities to use faith on behalf of ourselves and others.

---

49 Luke 10:19.
50 Mark 11:22, 23.

Jesus pointed out the reason why their faith failed. He said, "This kind can come out by nothing, save by prayer and fasting" (Mark 9:29, marginal reading included). This short statement is pregnant with truth:

1. Demons vary in "kind." Some are stronger than others. Demonic personalities are in this sense like people. Some men are physically stronger than others, and some are stronger in their wills. Some men will fight tenaciously against great odds and refuse to give up, while others will surrender after a token effort. Those experienced in deliverance ministry can readily testify of encountering demons with varying degrees of tenacity.

2. It requires more faith to cast out some demons than others. The deliverance minister can become satisfied with partial success. He may be able to cast out most demons at his level of faith, but should persist in faith until he is able to handle every demon he meets.

3. There are certain spiritual disciplines which are necessary to spiritual power. Prayer and fasting are keys to faith. These disciplines deny the flesh of its indulgences and priorities and turns one's full attention upon the Father and His Kingdom.

   Note: Jesus is not rebuking His disciples over their failure to fast. At this particular time the disciples were not required to fast.[51] Jesus is instructing the twelve and us. We are in that period of time when the Bridegroom is no longer present in this world, and we are to give ourselves to fasting.

No wonder the church and its ministers have become so faithless when so little attention has been given to prayer and fasting. God's children have forsaken the ways of God and perverted themselves by turning to the world and its fleshly indulgences. Such carnal lifestyles will never build strong men of faith.

---

51 Matthew 9:14, 15.

The Failure Rectified

The father appeals to the compassion of Jesus on behalf of his son. He asks Jesus if He can do anything to help, and Jesus immediately puts the responsibility on the father: "If thou canst! All things are possible to him that believeth." The compassion and ability of Jesus is not the question. The child's deliverance depends upon the father's faith.

Once again, as in the case of the Syrophonecian woman, we see a parent representing a child. The child receives deliverance based upon the faith of the parent. Children may need deliverance, and physical problems can be demonic. If so, they will not go away by themselves or by prayer alone. Whenever a demon is present, it must be cast out. If we have "the faith of God" (Mark 11:22, literal translation), we will be able to cast out every evil spirit. Let each of us say with the concerned father, "I believe; help thou mine unbelief" (Mark 9:24).

The demon put up a strong resistance, tore the boy, and left him lying lifeless upon the ground. A crowd had gathered and most of them thought the child was dead. As bizarre as this may sound to some, it is not an unusual experience in deliverance work. Strong spirits often put up demonstrative resistance, and the person is left weak and lifeless. But the person is not dead, and he soon recovers his strength and is perfectly normal.

EXCLUSIVENESS REBUKED

Mark 9:38-40; Luke 9:49-50

38 John said unto him, Teacher, we saw one
casting out demons in thy name; and we for-

39 bade him, because he followed not us. But
Jesus said, Forbid him not: for there is no
man which shall do a mighty work in my
name, and be able quickly to speak evil of me.

40 For he that is not against us is for us.

Some disciples of Jesus have a tendency to become like
the Apostle John, as reflected here in his attitude toward
other Christian workers, for they want to "corner the mar-
ket" and claim themselves the only ones qualified to minister deliverance. Unless others are identified with them
and their group they are judged to be in error. Such
pride-filled judgmentalism leads to exclusiveness.

Jesus rebuked such judgmentalism and exclusiveness.
He showed that we should encourage as many as possible
to be active in spiritual warfare. The devil continually
seeks to divide Christian workers against one another
through jealousy and by creating suspicion of one another's motives or methods. As long as others are doing miracles in the name of Jesus, they are to be counted as a
part of God's valid army.

The expression "mighty works" is rendered "miracles" in
other translations. It is the Greek word *dunamis* meaning
power, and is used concerning works of supernatural ori-

gin and character, such as could not be produced by natural agents and means. Thus, the casting out of demons is said by Jesus to be a miracle ministry.[52]

---

52 Compare Accts 8:6-11.

ENFORCING CHURCH DISCIPLINE

Matthew 18:15-18

15 And if thy brother sin against thee, go, shew him his fault between thee and him alone: if he hear thee, thou has gained thy brother.

16 But if he hear thee not, take with thee one or two more, that at the mouth of two witnesses

17 or three every word may be established. And if he refuse to hear them, tell it unto the church: and if he refuse to hear the church also, let him be unto thee as the Gentile and

18 the publican. Verily I say unto you, What things soever ye shall bind on earth shall be bound in heaven; and what things soever ye shall loose on earth shall be loosed in heaven.

There are only two times in the New Testament where Jesus used the word "church."[53] In both contexts Jesus immediately follows His reference to His Church by a declaration of His Church's power to bind and loose. In Matthew 16:18 the context is concerned with enemies outside of the Church: the gates of Hades which oppose the Church. In this second reference the context is concerned with division within the fellowship. If all efforts of

---

53 Matthew 16:18 and Matthew 18:17.

reconciliation end in failure, then the Church has spiritual authority to enforce its powers of excommunication over the unrepentant and uncooperative member.

> It is an awesome responsibility of Church authority to loose Satan to deal with those who refuse to submit to Church discipline.

Paul led the Church to use her authority on two occasions where the troublemakers could not be permitted to remain within the fellowship to corrupt the body or to disrupt the unity. They were turned over to Satan.[54]

The powers of Satan operating within a person can be bound, but the will of a person cannot be controlled by others. If the person himself continues to cause problems in the fellowship, Satan can be loosed to deal with such a person. This action is not to be taken until all other resources are exhausted to bring the sinner to repentance. It must be done under the direct leadership of the Holy Spirit. It is to be done ONLY by those with spiritual oversight in the Church (an apostolic responsibility). It is done in the authority of the Lord Jesus Christ and by the power to bind and loose given to the Church by Christ.[55]

---

54 I Corinthians 5:1-5; I Timothy 1:19, 20.
55 I Corinthians 5:4.

THE CURSE OF UNFORGIVENESS

Matthew 18:34,35

34 And his lord was wroth, and delivered him to the tormentors, till he should pay all that was due.

35 So shall also my heavenly Father do unto you, if ye forgive not every one his brother from your hearts.

Unconditional forgiveness of others is an absolute requirement for deliverance. The context, beginning in verse twenty three, couches the lesson of forgiveness in a parable based on a master-servant experience. The servant owed his master an insurmountable debt. There were no means by which he could ever hope to pay that debt. This typifies every man's sin debt, for there is no way by which any man can settle his own account with God.

The master is moved with compassion and forgives the debt, which typifies the compassion of Jesus in forgiving all our sins.

Next, we find that the forgiven servant refuses to forgive a fellow servant even a very small debt. The master is angry, and turns the unforgiving servant over to the tormentors till he shall pay the debt in full.

God requires those whom He has forgiven to be forgiving. If they are not, then He turns them over to "the tormentors" until they pay their debt of forgiveness.

God requires each of us to "Owe no man anything, save to love one another" (Romans 13:8). We all owe a debt of love which can only be paid through forgiveness. There will always be offenses, so there will always be the need to forgive others. This is one debt that we had better keep "paid up".

Demon spirits are tormentors, and they are the tormentors to whom God turns a person over when they refuse to forgive others.

> When God turns one over to the torment of evil spirits, these tormenting demons cannot be cast out until the person wills to forgive those who have trespassed against him.

Otherwise, the demons have a legal right to be there, for God has given them permission.

The one suffering the torment of evil spirits may experience torment of mind, emotions, or physical body. This is why the deliverance minister should always lead the person seeking deliverance in a prayer by which he forgives, by an act of his will, each person who has ever wronged him.

The author has seen many examples of unforgiving persons remain in their torment and receive no deliverance until they met God's condition. God requires forgiveness of all others, irregardless of the circumstances.

Sometimes a person feels justified in harboring bitterness towards another. He considers his hurt too severe to warrant forgiveness. But, when he honestly considers what Jesus has done to forgive him, he will be put to shame for his UNFORGIVENESS.

THE MISSION OF
THE SEVENTY

Luke 10:1, 17-20

1 Now after these things the Lord appointed
seventy others, and sent them two and two
before his face into every city and place,
whither he himself was about to come...

17 And the seventy returned with joy, saying,
Lord, even the demons are subject unto us

18 in thy name. And he said unto them, I beheld
Satan fallen as lightning from heaven.

19 Behold, I have given you authority to tread
upon serpents and scorpions, and over all the
power of the enemy: and nothing shall in any

20 wise hurt you. Nevertheless in this rejoice
not, that the spirits are subject unto you; but
rejoice that your names are written in heaven.

The Need For Laborers

The commissioning of the seventy should be compared
with that of the twelve.[56] In both passages Jesus calls
attention to the waiting harvest and the shortage of laborers. In both instances He urges His disciples to pray for
more laborers, and then He sends His disciples two by
two into those very fields.

---

56 Matthew 9:36-10:1.

The need for more laborers for Christ has never diminished. The urgency of filling the spiritual harvest fields with laborers has intensified in our day and time. The cry for deliverance workers is especially acute. There are more needs than are being met. Many countries around the world are crying out for someone to come over to their "Macedonia" and help them.

> In every instance where Jesus commissioned disciples to go forth, He gave them authority to cast out demons:

(1) The twelve. Matthew 10:1,8
(2) The seventy. Luke 10:1,17
(3) The church. Mark 16:17

When He sent out the twelve, the first power granted them was to cast out unclean spirits. When the seventy returned, the first success reported was that demons were subject to them through His name. When Jesus commissioned the church, He said that supernatural signs will follow believers. The first sign mentioned is: "in my name shall ye cast out demons". These "first" mentions are indicative of the priority that deliverance should be given by those who go forth to preach the gospel.

Giving God the Glory

The seventy gave God the glory for their victories. All was done in the name of Jesus. God will honor His servants, but He will not share His glory with another. We must be quick to give God all the glory, for no victory over Satan is ever won apart from His name.

Satan's Defeat Confirmed

Jesus confirmed their report. His eye was upon them as they went forth. He knew their successes for He "beheld Satan fallen as lightning from heaven". He saw Satan's kingdom thrown down and the Kingdom of God established in its place.

Satan's being cast down is always followed by the coming in of God's Kingdom.

> And the great dragon was cast down, the old serpent, he that is called the Devil and Satan, the deceiver of the whole world; he was cast down to the earth, and his angels were cast down with him. And I heard a great voice in heaven, saying, NOW IS COME THE SALVATION, AND THE POWER, AND THE KINGDOM OF OUR GOD, AND THE AUTHORITY OF HIS CHRIST: FOR THE ACCUSER OF OUR BRETHREN IS CAST DOWN...
>
> Revelation 12:9-10

This casting down of Satan from his position of control, and replacing him with the Lordship of Christ, is reenacted each time a successful deliverance is experienced.

The Believer's Authority

The disciples were reminded of the authority given them. They shall "tread upon serpents and scorpions". That is, they received dominion over both the greater and lesser ranks of evil spirits. Serpents are more venomous than scorpions and represent more powerful demons. Too, serpents and scorpions may also refer to different types of demons. Throughout scripture the serpent is associated with deception, and the scorpion is a type of fear and torment. In either case,

believers are given authority over "all" the minions of Satan.

While the believer is putting Satan under his feet he is comforted by the promise of the Lord that "nothing shall in any wise hurt you". Surely the devil would hurt us if he could, but he is unable to retaliate when attacked. This promise of immunity from hurt must not lead us into presumption or carelessness, for we must ever have on the "whole armor of God" (Ephesians 6:11) as we engage in spiritual battle. The enemy is able to take advantage of any exposed areas where the armor of God is not in place. In fact, demons enter through openings created by the omission of any part of one's spiritual armor.

The promise that "nothing shall in any wise hurt you" gives us boldness to engage in spiritual battle against demons which indwell individuals and against territorial principalities in heavenly places.

> We have the assurance of God's Word that we will not be hurt by the devil when we tread upon him.

The Grounds For Rejoicing

Surely, each victory over the devil is ground for rejoicing, yet as glorious as these victories are they are not the primary cause for rejoicing. The power that makes one a child of God[57] is of greater consequence than the power to cast out demons.

There are some who will have cast out demons who will be disowned by Christ in the day of judgment,[58] but all whose names are written in the Lamb's Book of Life will live eternally.

Before, during and after a time of deliverance it is good to rejoice in the Lord and praise him exuberantly. Let each one present give thanks for the honor and blessing of being God's child and having his name recorded in heaven.

---

57 John 1:12.
58 Matthew 7:21-23.

A SPIRIT OF INFIRMITY

Luke 13:10-17

10 And he was teaching in one of the synagogues

11 on the sabbath day. And behold, a woman which had a spirit of infirmity eighteen years; and she was bowed together, and could in no

12 wise lift herself up. And when Jesus saw her, he called her, and said to her, Woman, thou art

13 loosed from thine infirmity. And he laid his hands upon her: and immediately she was

14 made straight, and glorified God. And the ruler of the synagogue, being moved with indignation because Jesus had healed on the sabbath, answered and said to the multitude, There are six days in which men ought to work: in them therefore come and be healed,

15 and not on the day of the sabbath. But the Lord answered him, and said, Ye hypocrites, doth not each one of you on the sabbath loose his ox or his ass from the stall, and lead him

16 away to watering? And ought not this woman, being a daughter of Abraham, whom Satan had bound, lo, these eighteen years, to have been loosed from this bond on the day of the

17 sabbath? And as he said these things, all his adversaries were put to shame: and all the

multitude rejoiced for all the glorious things
that were done by him.

Christians Need Deliverance

The scene of this mighty deliverance is in a synagogue,
the place where God's people met each sabbath to worship and be taught the Word of God. The woman with the
"spirit of infirmity" was one of the worshippers. In like
manner today, the need for deliverance is often found
among the most devoted of worshippers. This should
come as no surprise.[59]

Demons Cause Infirmities

Some infirmities are caused by evil spirits. This poor
woman had been bound in her body for eighteen years.
She was unable to stand erect, and was probably in pain.
Think of the spectrum of medical treatments and medica-
tions to which she would have been subjected in our day!
But the simple remedy for her problem was deliverance.

Jesus cast out spirits of blindness, muteness, deafness,
epilepsy and fever. Much of the healing which Jesus did
was through deliverance or in conjunction with deliverance. The same is true today. Tumors, seizures, high
blood pressure, asthma, barrenness, warts, cancer, dia-
betes, blindness, deafness and many other physical mal-
adies are seen cured through deliverance.

> Not every disease and infirmity of the body rep-
> resents a clear-cut deliverance need.

Remember that Jesus healed many people when there
is no mention of deliverance. Let us not falter in faith
when a needed healing is not experienced through deliverance. Jesus is both Deliverer and Healer!

---

59 Mark 1:21-28.

Manifestations Not Always Evidenced

There is no mention of manifestations when the infirmity demon was cast out of the woman. There probably were none, for this is the case with many out of whom evil spirits are cast. Manifestations do not always accompany deliverance, although manifestations are a common occurrence.

Loosed From Demons

Jesus "loosed" this woman whom Satan had bound. This gives us insight into the words of Jesus when he spoke of the keys of the Kingdom by which we have power to loose.[60] What needs to be loosed? Those whom Satan has bound need loosing. Jesus has given us power to bind Satan and loose the captives.

Laying On Of Hands

"And he laid his hands upon her." Jesus often laid His hands upon those to whom He ministered. This practice is found to be helpful in deliverance, although it is not always necessary. As in all ministry situations, one should be led of the Holy Spirit rather than be restricted by standardized methods.

> There should be no fear of getting another's demons by laying one's hands upon a person when ministering deliverance.

Remember that demons can only enter through open doors. If the deliverance minister has opened no door of opportunity to the evil spirit, none can enter him.

The Bread Is For God's Children

The woman was "a daughter of Abraham," which entitled her to the blessings of the Messiah. She was spiritu-

---

60 Matthew 16:19.

ally qualified to partake of "the children's bread" (Mark 7:27).

Also, being "a daughter of Abraham" meant that she was a "sister" to the ruler of the synagogue and the Jews who were insensitive to her infirmity. She meant less to them than to an ox or an ass who fared better under their sabbath regulations.

> People are a priority with Jesus, and they should be a priority with the Church.

When religious rules and regulations become more important than people and their needs, then heartless legalism takes precedence over love and compassion.

Objections Raised By Religious Leaders

Once again there was objection to what Jesus did. The ruler of the synagogue was offended when Jesus healed on the sabbath and thereby disregarded a Jewish legalistic tradition. When Jesus bluntly rebuked their hypocrisy, His adversaries were put to shame. Sooner or later all religionists who despise and oppose Christ's miracles of healing and deliverance will be made ashamed.

Their hypocrisy was transparent. They hated Christ and cloaked their hatred in a pretended zeal for the Sabbath. A spirit of Antichrist controlled these Jews. It is the spirit of Antichrist that denies the deity and supernatural works of Christ.

ATTEMPTED INTIMIDATION

Luke 13:31-32

31 In that very hour there came certain Pharisees, saying to him, Get thee out, and go

32 hence: for Herod would fain kill thee. And he
   said unto them, Go and say to that fox,
   Behold, I cast out demons and perform cures
   to-day and to- morrow, and the third day I
   am perfected.

The Pharisees sought to frighten Jesus by warning Him
of King Herod's intentions to kill Him. Jesus let it be
known that He would continue His ministry of deliverance
and healing until He went to the cross.

The devil has not ceased his intimidation tactics. Today
he whispers fear in the ears of pastors and church leaders. This is Satan's attempt to stop the ministries of healing and deliverance. In the original Greek, both Herod and
the Pharisee who warned Jesus to flee were called "foxes".
The text reads, "Go, and tell that fox, yea, and this fox
too..."

Fear is the primary reason why more Christian leaders
are not following Christ's commission to cast out demons.
There is the fear of demon retaliation, fear of denominational leaders, fear of other's opinions, fear of losing
church members, fear of confrontation, fear of failure, fear
of criticism and fear of imbalance.

Jesus did not flinch when threatened. He knew that His
enemies could do him no harm. His destiny was to fulfil
the Father's will. He would die in Jerusalem on the cross.

In order to withstand Satan's intimidating tactics the man of God much possess three qualities:

1. CONVICTION
    (1) That deliverance is scriptural — a provision of the cross. (Matthew 8:16,17).
    (2) That nothing can substitute for deliverance — neither counseling, teaching or "faith only".
    (3) That to avoid or withstand deliverance is to oppose Jesus Christ. (Matthew 12:30)
2. COMMITMENT
    (1) To endure the physical demands of long hours because of the press of the crowd and the need to persist in warfare until victory comes.
    (2) To endure patiently with those who need repeated help.
    (3) To endure the repulsive manifestations of unclean spirits.
    (4) To meet the spiritual requirements of prayer, fasting and keeping oneself free.
    (5) To love the unloved and unlovely, being a friend and keeping confidentialities.
3. COURAGE
    (1) To confront the devil and his demons.
    (2) To obey God in the face of criticism.
    (3) To stand strong in the face of threats and intimidations.

The servant of God must be alert to every attempt to turn him aside from God's calling.

SATAN ENTERS INTO JUDAS

Luke 22:3-4

3 And Satan entered into Judas who was called
   Iscariot, being of the number of the twelve.
4 And he went away, and communed with the
   chief priests and captains, how he might
   deliver him unto them.

Satan Works Through People

Satan uses men to accomplish his purposes. Through
deceit he enlists them as his agents. Jesus had chosen
Judas as one of The Twelve, and Jesus knew from the
beginning what was in Judas's heart, for He said: "Did not I
choose you the twelve, and one of you is a devil? He spake
of Judas the son of Simon Iscariot, for he it was that
should betray him, being one of the twelve" (John 6:70-71).

Satan Enters Judas

It has been a matter of debate among students of scripture as to whether Satan himself entered into Judas, or
whether a demon spirit indwelt him. Some have conjec-
tured that Satan would not leave this key responsibility to
any lesser spirit than himself. Others see Satan as the
supreme authority over the demonic kingdom, who always
works through his "angels", or messengers, to accomplish
his purposes.

Satan is a fallen angel, "the anointed cherub that cov-
ereth" Ezekiel 28:14. In all probability he was an arch
angel. When Satan led his rebellion in heaven he drew a
third of the "stars" (angels) with him (see: Revelation 12:4).

These fallen angels make up the principalities, powers, world rulers and wicked spirituals whose sphere of operation is in "heavenly places" (Ephesians 6:12).

There is a distinction between fallen angels and demons. Throughout scripture angels are consistently represented as having their own bodies. On the other hand, demons are spirits without bodies. Demon spirits seek bodies, preferably the bodies of humans, to inhabit in order to carry out their evil purposes. Angels, having their own bodies, do not indwell men's bodies.

When Judas betrayed Christ, it was Satan who instigated it. Metaphorically speaking, when a demon-agent from Satan entered into Judas it was said, "and Satan entered into Judas."

Sin Opens The Door

Judas was covetous and took advantage of his position as treasurer of the group to pilfer from the funds.[61] Satan used the avarice in Judas' heart to tempt him to gain a few pieces of silver through betraying Jesus. As always, Satan's appealing temptations soon become bitter curses. The one who comes "that he may steal, and kill, and destroy" (John 10:10), gained another victim.

Judas Was "A Devil"

Jesus had said that Judas was "a devil" (John 6:70). The word "devil" (Greek: diabolos) means accuser; slanderer. That is, Judas maliciously made false charges against Jesus that were calculated to damage Christ's reputation. All who enter into such character assassination against others have submitted themselves to the same spirit to which Judas yielded.

"Devil" is one of the names of Satan. He is THE devil. Judas is the only person throughout the Bible who is said to be "a devil". That is, Judas was like the devil himself; Judas was an accuser, a liar, a hypocrite. Judas not only had a demon but was a devil. His character was false.

The case with Judas enables us to understand why deliverance from demons is not an instant cure for every prob-

---

61 John 12:6.

lem. If Judas' problem had been simply demonic, Jesus would have cast out the demon(s) and set him free. Judas' heart was not right. He needed a change from within.

If a person is basically evil, he opens himself up for demons to indwell. A flawed character is a door through which demons enter. Along with deliverance a man must develop integrity — purity, honesty and uprightness — otherwise demons have a legal right to remain.

We might also ask, "Why did not Jesus cast demons out of the Pharisees and set them free from their hypocrisy and judgmentalism"? Because they would not accept His word. They would not admit their need to change. They were unteachable. This is why Jesus said to them, "ye are of your father the devil" (John 8:44).

A true child of God will bear the characteristics of his Father. He will be holy. At least he will be striving for holiness. Those who portray the nature and character of the devil have no grounds for boasting that either God or Abraham is their Father.

SATAN ASKS FOR PETER

Luke 22:31-32

31 Simon, Simon, behold, Satan asked to have

32 you, that he might sift you as wheat: but I
made supplication for thee, that thy faith fail
not; and do thou, when once thou hast
turned again, establish thy brethren.

Satan had come to Jesus requesting permission to
assault and afflict all of the apostles. The "you" is plural.
Satan wanted to get at them all, but especially Peter.
Peter was the usual spokesman for the rest and the more
forward and impulsive of them all.

> Satan makes it a priority to capture spiritual
> leaders, for he knows that when leaders fall, they
> affect the lives of many others.

Satan Is Limited

Satan's request is reminiscent of his request to try
Job.[62] His power is limited by God's sovereign grace. If it
were not for God's protection, Satan would have destroyed
each of us long ago. And even as God permitted Satan to
test Job, Jesus permitted Satan to test His chosen disci-

---

62 Job 1:6-12.

ples. Through this "sifting," He knew that they would be refined. Satan meant it for evil, but God meant it for good.

Satan's intention was to demonstrate that there was nothing but chaff in Peter, but Jesus knew that when Peter saw how much chaff was in him, he would repent and then become more effective in ministering to others.

Christ Our Intercessor

Peter was given encouragement through Christ's assurance of special intercession for him as he underwent this trial of his faith. Which one of us would invite trials into his own life? If the choice were left to us, we would always choose immunity from difficulties. A few years later, after Peter had this trial behind him, he wrote:

> Beloved, think it not strange concerning the fiery trial among you, which cometh upon you to prove you, as though a strange thing happened unto you: but insomuch as ye are partakers of Christ's sufferings, rejoice; that at the revelation of his glory also ye may rejoice with exceeding joy.
>
> I Peter 4:12-13

Notice how Jesus prayed for Peter. He prayed that his faith would not fail. It is the shield of faith which quenches all the fiery darts of the evil one.[63] Fear is a fiery dart that only faith can quench. Fear is defeated by faith. Satan cast fear at Peter; and when Peter was confronted by a young woman as to his association with Jesus, he was gripped with fear that he too might be put to death. This fear caused him to deny his Lord.

There can be a temporary lapse of faith, which is different from a total failure of faith. Peter was sustained by the intercession of Jesus from complete disaster. It is comforting to realize that Jesus intercedes for each of us personally. He also has taught us to pray for ourselves: "And do not lead us into temptation, But deliver us from the evil one" (Luke 11:4, New King James).

---

63 Ephesians 6:16.

Establish Your Brethren

Jesus let Peter know that he had a specific ministry which awaited him on the other side of the trial. After he had been tested and recovered through repentance, he could then strengthen his brethren.

In order to be effectively used by the Lord, we need to be purged vessels. As the dross is removed from our lives, we can more readily minister to others. We, like Peter, may feel that we are strong, and that we would never deny our Lord. The testings reveal the chaff. When our chaff is exposed, we should be brought to repentance and restoration of relationship with Jesus. Then we can serve him by ministering to others.

The motive in seeking deliverance is to be free from every hindrance to serving the Lord and to ministering to others in His name.

After David had fallen to the Tempter's stroke, he prayed:

> Hide thy face from my sins,
> And blot out all mine iniquities.
> Create in me a clean heart, O God:
> And renew a right spirit within me.
> Cast me not away from thy presence;
> And take not thy holy Spirit from me.
> Restore unto me the joy of thy salvation;
> And uphold me with a willing spirit.
> Then will I teach transgressors thy ways;
> And sinners shall be converted unto thee.
>
> Psalm 51:9-13.
>
> Amen!

Frank HAMMOND, Author of *PIGS IN THE PARLOR* amplifies and expands the teachings of this important book in several series of cassettes. In these tapes he reveals additional truths gleaned from his own far reaching ministry in the area of deliverance and related fields. Much needed truth and light is to be gained from his rich insights and down-to-earth teaching. (4.95 each)

DELIVERANCE SERIES:
___4.95___HEALING THE PERSONALITY
___4.95___THE SCHIZOPHRENIA REVELATION I
___4.95___THE SCHIZOPHRENIA REVELATION 2
___4.95___MAINTAINING DELIVERANCE
___4.95___DEALING WITH PRESSURES
___4.95___THE ARM OF THE FLESH

FREEDOM FROM BONDAGE SERIES:
___4.95___ESCAPE INTO BONDAGE
___4.95___BONDAGE TO SIN
___4.95___BONDAGE TO SELF
___4.95___BONDAGE TO MAN
___4.95___BREAKING OF CURSES
___4.95___FLESH VS. SPIRIT

END-TIME SERIES:
___4.95___END-TIME BEHAVIOR (PART I)
___4.95___END TIME BEHAVIOR (PART II)
___4.95___END-TIME BEHAVIOR (PART III)
___4.95___END-TIME BEHAVIOR (PART IV)
___4.95___THE CHRISTIAN & TRIBULATION
___4.95___THE UNRIGHTEOUSNESS &
                    GOD'S WRATH

MESSAGES ON LOVE SERIES:
___4.95___FRIENDSHIP
___4.95___MY BROTHER'S KEEPER
___4.95___THE PERFECTING OF LOVE
___4.95___LEARNING TO LOVE
___4.95___REMEMBERING TO FORGET

WALK IN THE SPIRIT SERIES:
___4.95___FUNCTIONING AS SPIRITUAL MEN
___4.95___SPIRITUAL PERCEPTION
___4.95___SEEING INTO THE SPIRITUAL REALM
___4.95___THE FRUIT OF RIGHTEOUSNESS
___4.95___WHAT ADVANTAGE MY
                    RIGHTEOUSNESS?
___4.95___THE MINISTRY OF EDIFICATION

FAITH SERIES:
___4.95___THINGS THAT DESTROY FAITH
___4.95___THINGS THAT ENCOURAGE FAITH
___4.95___THE LANGUAGE OF FAITH
___4.95___CORRESPONDING ACTION OF FAITH
___4.95___THE DEVELOPMENT OF FAITH
___4.95___PRAYING THE PRAYERS OF PAUL

CHURCH SERIES:
___4.95___THE BODY OF CHRIST
___4.95___THE FAMILY OF GOD
___4.95___THE TEMPLE OF GOD
___4.95___GOD'S HUSBANDRY
___4.95___THE ARMY OF GOD
___4.95___THE BRIDE OF CHRIST

SPIRITUAL MEAT SERIES:
___4.95___THE LORD'S SUPPER
___4.95___DISCERNING THE LORD'S BODY
___4.95___WORSHIP & PRAISE
___4.95___WHAT DEFILES A MAN?
___4.95___STABILIZE
___4.95___KNOWING WHO YOU ARE AS A
                    BELIEVER

FAMILY IN THE KINGDOM SERIES:
___4.95___THE HUSBAND'S HEADSHIP
___4.95___THE WIFE'S SUBMISSION
___4.95___THE WIFE'S INFLUENCE
___4.95___BRINGING UP CHILDREN (PART 1)
___4.95___BRINGING UP CHILDREN (PART 2)
___4.95___THE WIFE'S SANCTIFICATION
                    (IDA MAE HAMMOND)

RECOGNIZING GOD SERIES:
___4.95___GOD OUR SOURCE
___4.95___GOD OUR PROVIDER
___4.95___GOD OUR REFUGE

SPECIAL PRICE OFFER:
The entire set of above Hammond tapes is offered for just $224.00. (Save over $53.00) Each individual tape is $4.95. Or, just buy 5, and 6th tape is free!

FOR THOSE SEEKING MORE INFORMATION...
...ABOUT DEMONOLGY & DELIVERANCE

Banks, Bill

___BREAKING UNHEALTHY SOUL-TIES	P	7.95
___MINISTERING TO ABORTION'S AFTERMATH	P	5.95
___POWER FOR DELIVERANCE (Songs of Deliverance)	P	5.95
___DELIVERANCE FOR CHILDREN & TEENS	P	6.95
___DELIVERANCE FROM CHILDLESSNESS	P	5.95
___DELIVERANCE FROM FAT	P	5.95
___SHAME-FREE	P	7.95

Basham, Don

___CAN A CHRISTIAN HAVE A DEMON?	P	5.95
___DELIVER US FROM EVIL	P	12.00

Garrison, Mary

____BINDING & LOOSING	P	6.99
____HOW TO TRY A SPIRIT	P	6.99
____HOW TO CONDUCT SPIRITUAL WARFARE	P	6.99

Hagin, Kenneth

____THE TRIUMPHANT CHURCH	P	9.95

Hammond, Frank

____BREAKING OF CURSES	P	6.00
____COMFORT FOR THE WOUNDED SPIRIT	P	5.95
____DEMONS & DELIVERANCE	P	6.00
____PIGS IN THE PARLOR	P	7.95
____KINGDOM LIVING FOR THE FAMILY	P	6.95
____MANUAL FOR CHILDREN'S DELIVERANCE	P	7.95
____OVERCOMING REJECTION	P	5.95
____SAINTS AT WAR	P	5.95
____SOUL TIES (Booklet)	P	3.00
____FAMILIAR SPIRITS (Booklet)	P	3.00

Lindsay, Gordon

____JOHN G. LAKE SERMONS ON DOMINION OVER		
DEMONS, DISEASE AND DEATH	P	5.95
____SATAN AND HIS KINGDOM OF DARKNESS	P	9.95

Prince, Derek

____EXPELLING DEMONS	P	1.50
____SPIRITUAL WARFARE	P	7.99

— CASSETTE SERIES ON DELIVERANCE —

____6001 HOW I CAME TO GRIPS WITH DEMONS	C	5.95
____6002 HOW JESUS DEALT WITH DEMONS	C	5.95
____6003 NATURE AND ACTIVITY OF DEMONS	C	5.95
____6004 HOW TO RECOGNIZE & EXPEL DEMONS	C	5.95
____6005 CULT & OCCULT: SATAN'S SNARES	C	5.95
____6006 7 WAYS TO KEEP YOUR DELIVERANCE	C	5.95
____6007 Teenagers: Youth's Place and Problems in the End-times	C	5.95
____6008 Children (5-11) Instructions on Deliverance for Children & Parent	C	5.95
____SET OF 6001 - 6006 ..... SPECIAL	30.50	
____SET OF 6001 - 6008 ..... SPECIAL	40.50	

**SAVE $57.26 - Entire Set of Above Books & Tapes ONLY $171.00
**SAVE $46.70 - Entire Set of Books (No Tapes) ONLY $136.00

... ABOUT THE ENEMY AND OUR ROLE

Banks, William

____BREAKING UNHEALTY SOUL-TIES	P	7.95
____DELIVERANCE FOR CHILDREN	P	6.95
____MINISTERING TO ABORTION'S AFTERMATH	P	5.95
____POWER FOR DELIVERANCE (Songs of Deliverance)	P	5.95
____SHAME- FREE	P	7.95

Hagin, Kenneth

____THE BELIEVER'S AUTHORITY	P	4.95

White, Anne

____TRIAL BY FIRE	P	3.95

SAVE $7.70 - Entire Set of Books ONLY $30.00

... ABOUT THE BAPTISM OF THE HOLY SPIRIT

Banks, Bill
____ALIVE AGAIN! P 5.95
Basham, Don
____HANDBOOK ON HOLY SPIRIT BAPTISM P 7.99
Delgado, Gabriele
____A LOVE STORY P 1.25
Gilles, George & Harriett
____SCRIPTURAL OUTLINE of the Baptism in the Holy Spirit P 4.99
Hagin, Kenneth
____SEVEN VITAL STEPS TO RECEIVING THE H.S. P 3.95
Lindsay, Gordon
____COMMISSIONED WITH POWER P14.95
Prince, Derek
____BAPTISM IN THE HOLY SPIRIT P 7.99
Sherrill, John
____THEY SPEAK WITH OTHER TONGUES P 8.99

SAVE $ 10.56 - Entire Set of Books ONLY $38.50

... ABOUT GROWING IN SPIRIT AND FAITH

Banks, Bill
____ALIVE AGAIN! P 5.95
____THE HEAVENS DECLARE P 8.95
____HOW TO TAP INTO THE WISDOM OF GOD P 10.95
Brant, Roxanne
__✓ MINISTERING TO THE LORD P 7.99
Buess, Bob
__✓ FAVOR, THE ROAD TO SUCCESS P 5.99
Carothers, Merlin
__✓ POWER IN PRAISE P 6.95
Hagin, Kenneth
____HOW TO TURN YOUR FAITH LOOSE P 3.95
____WHAT FAITH IS P 3.95
Johnson, Gordon D.
____THE GLORIOUS CROSS OF ST. JOHN P 8.95
Jones, Russell B.
____GOLD FROM GOLGOTHA P 1.50
Miller, Basil
____GEORGE MUELLER P 4.99
Trumbull, H.C.
____THE BLOOD COVENANT P 12.95
____THE SALT COVENANT P 12.95
____THE THRESHOLD COVENANT P 12.95
Wigglesworth, Smith
____EVERINCREASING FAITH P 4.99
____FAITH THAT PREVAILS P 4.99
Whyte, Maxwell
____THE POWER OF THE BLOOD P 5.99

SAVE $23.94 - Entire Set of Books ONLY $100.00

. . . ABOUT HEALING FROM GOD

Alsobrook, David
___ ✓ JESUS CHRIST,M.D. The Healing Min of Jesus of Naz.   P 6.95

Banks, Bill
___ ALIVE AGAIN!   P 5.95
___ HOW I WAS HEALED OF CANCER & BAPTISED IN
        THE HOLY SPIRIT - (1 hr. cassette)   C 4.95
___ THREE KINDS OF FAITH FOR HEALING. . .   P 4.95
___ DELIVERANCE FROM CHILDLESSNESS   P 5.95
___ OVERCOMING BLOCKS TO HEALING   P 9.95

Bosworth, F.F.
___ CHRIST THE HEALER   P10.99

Hagin, Kenneth
___ HEALING BELONGS TO US   P 3.95
___ KEYS TO SCRIPTURAL HEALING   P 3.95

Lindsay, Gordon
    SERIES ON DIVINE HEALING & HEALTH
___ BIBLE SECRET OF DIVINE HEALTH   P 3.25
___ HOW YOU CAN BE HEALED   P 2.95
___ REAL REASON WHY CHRISTIANS ARE SICK   P 3.95
___ 30 BIBLE REASONS WHY CHRIST HEALS TODAY   P 3.50
___ 25 OBJECTIONS TO DIVINE HEALING & ANS   P 1.95
___ DIFFICULT QUESTIONS ON DIVINE HEALING   P 1.95
___ ....SET OF ABOVE SERIES (7 Titles)   ....SET 15.00

LAKE, John G.
___ SERMS/ DOM. OVER DEMONS, DISEASE, DEATH   P 5.95

SAVE $21.09 - Entire Set of Books ONLY $60.00

===

TOTAL QUANTITY _____ **TOTAL ORDER** _____

Missouri Residents add 7% Sales Tax _____
Minimum Postage $4.00 for one book:
PLUS .30 for each additional item _____
TOTAL AMOUNT ENCLOSED _____

NAME:_____Address_____
City_____St.____Zip_____Date_____
Credit Card #_____Exp/Date_____

Prices subject to change.
Write for complete catalog of over 600 Christian Books
IMPACT CHRISTIAN BOOKS, INC.
332 Leffingwell, Suite #101, Kirkwood, MO 63122

You may visit our Website at ***impactchristianbooks.com***
You may FAx an order with credit card information to 1-314-822-3325.
You may also e-mail an order with credit card information to
impactchristianbooks@Juno.com

CERDOS EN LA SALA

More than 500,000 copies of PIGS IN THE PARLOR, the recognized hand-book of Deliverance, are continuing to help set people free around the world from demonic bondages. This Bestseller is now also available IN SPANISH — at the same price as the English edition.

Paperback 7.95

KINGDOM LIVING FOR THE FAMILY

A long awaited sequel to PIGS IN THE PARLOR, offering not mere unrealistic theories, but rather a Practical Plan for implementing divine order in the family, and preventing the need for deliverance.

Paperback 6.95

OVERCOMING REJECTION

Powerful help for confronting and dealing with rejection, which so often is found to be a root in individuals requiring deliverance. This book will help understand a tool commonly employed by the enemy in his attacks upon believers.

Paperback 5.95

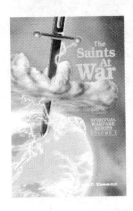

THE SAINTS AT WAR

Too many Christian Soldiers are remaining inactive and ineffective in this hour of battle. This book is both a "call to arms" and an instruction manual to enable the Church, God's Army, to become aggressively militant toward its enemy, and that all the Saints of God might become SAINTS AT WAR.

Paperback 5.95

Booklets:

GOD WARNS AMERICA

In a night vision the author was shown three terrible judgments to come upon America: economic, bloodshed, and persecution of the Church. God reveals why and what must be done to avert the outpouring of His wrath.

Booklet 3.00

FAMILIAR SPIRITS

Brief, simple, but helpful scriptural information on this category of spirits and how to deal with them.

Booklet 3.00

SOUL TIES

Are a reality. Booklet explains what must be done to break them.

Booklet 3.00

Please send minimum postage of $1.50 plus 30¢ per book with your order.

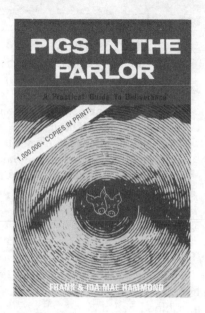

PIGS IN THE
PARLOR

A Practical Guide To Deliverance

1,000,000+ COPIES IN PRINT!

FRANK & IDA MAE HAMMOND

Bestseller!!

PIGS IN THE PARLOR
$7.95

If you *really believe* JESUS delivered people from evil spirits . . . Then you owe it to yourself to read this book! Learn that it *still happens today!*

This book contains a wealth of practical information for the person **interested in, planning to engage in, or actively engaged in** the ministry of deliverance.

It is a PRACTICAL HANDBOOK, offering valuable guidance as to determining . . .

- **HOW DEMONS ENTER** • **IF DELIVERANCE IS NEEDED** • **HOW DELIVERANCE IS ACCOMPLISHED FOR OTHERS AND SELF** • **HOW TO RETAIN DELIVERANCE** • **GROUPINGS OF DEMONS** (listing those demons that are often found together).

The book also includes a chapter presenting a revelation on the problems of **SCHIZOPHRENIA** which could well revolutionize the way this subject has been traditionally viewed by the medical profession!

IMPACT CHRISTIAN BOOKS, INC.

Announces

The Exciting New Power for Deliverance Series:

Power for Deliverance; Songs of Deliverance
Power for Deliverance From Fat
Power for Deliverance for Children
Power for Deliverance From Childlessness

Lives have already been changed by the powerful truths and revelations contained in these books as the author has taught them over the past seventeen years. These deliverance tools have been tested in the crucible of prayer room battles to free lives from Satan's control. You have tasted in this book the kind of dramatic accounts and truths which are to be found in the other volumes in this series.

Each book is just $5.95. When ordering, add $1.50 postage and handling for the first book and $.50 for each additional title.

Available at your local Christian bookstore, library,
or directly from:

Impact Christian Books, Inc.
332 Leffingwell Avenue, Suite 101
Kirkwood, MO 63122

Are you aware that demonic spirits can prevent childbirth?

DELIVERANCE FROM CHILDLESSNESS

During the first year this book was in print eight babies were conceived by women formerly diagnosed as "incapable of having children!"

This book offers the first real hope for certain childless couples...because, for some, there is a **spiritual** rather than a physical block preventing conception.

The testimonies included will build your faith as will the Scriptural truths revealed. Surprisingly the Scripture says quite a bit about childlessness and gives:
* reports of at least 9 unexpected or miraculous births granted to formerly childless or barren mothers;
* examples of women who were healed of barrenness;
* children granted in answer to prayer;
* instances of children denied because of *a curse of childlessness*

You will also learn:
* How curses of childlessness come into being, and how they may be broken.
* Ways that spirits of infertility and sterility enter, and how to cast them out.

Deliverance From Childlessness $5.95
Plus $1.50 shipping and handling.

THE HEAVENS DECLARE . . .
William D. Banks

More than 250 pages!
More than 50 illustrations!

- Who named the stars and why?
- What were the original names of the stars?
- What is the secret message hidden in the stars?

The surprising, **secret message** contained in the earliest, original names of the stars, is revealed in this new book.

The deciphering of the star names provides a fresh revelation from the heart of **the intelligence** behind creation. Ten years of research includes material from the British Museum dating prior to 2700 B.C.

A clear explanation is given showing that early man had a sophisticated knowledge of One, True God!

$8.95 + $1.75 Shipping/Handling

ALIVE AGAIN!
William D. Banks

The author, healed over twenty years ago, relates his own story. His own testimony presents a miracle or really a series of miracles — as seen through the eyes of a doubting skeptic, who himself becomes the object of the greatest miracle, because he is Alive Again!

The way this family pursues and finds divine healing as well as a great spiritual blessing provides a story that will at once bless you, refresh you, restore your faith or challenge it! You will not be the same after you have read this true account of the healing gospel of Jesus Christ, and how He is working in the world today.

The healing message contained in this book needs to be heard by every cancer patient, every seriously ill person, and by every Christian hungering for the reality of God.

More than a powerful testimony — here is teaching which can introduce you or those whom you love to healing and to a new life in the Spirit!

$5.95 + $1.75 Shipping/Handling

THREE KINDS OF FAITH FOR HEALING

Many today have been taught that the only way to be healed is to personally have faith for their healing. It is implied, one must somehow 'work up' or develop enough personal *faith-to-be-healed,* and then healing will come. Many have also been told that the reason they remain afflicted is because of their lack of faith.

Such statements in addition to being utterly devoid of compassion, are terribly devastating to the poor hearers. One could never imagine Jesus saying something so heartless. Yet these things are often said today. Even those who have not heard these words spoken aloud have received them through implication from proud, spiritually 'superior' friends who believe that these sick individuals are somehow deficient in faith.

There is good news both for them and for us, because that teaching is wrong. There are more ways of being healed than just the one way, as we have been taught.

In this new book, Bill Banks presents a *revelation* of three main types of faith for healing illustrated in Scripture, and a fourth which is a combination of the other three.

Three Kinds of Faith For Healing   **Paper 4.95**

POWERFUL NEW BOOK

MINISTERING TO
ABORTION'S AFTERMATH

Bill and Sue Banks

This new book is unique because it offers real help for the suffering women who have already had abortions. This book is full of GOOD NEWS!

It shows how to minister to them, or may be used by the women themselves as it contains simple steps to self-ministry.

Millions of women **have had abortions:** every one of them is a potential candidate for the type of ministry presented in this book. Every minister, every counsellor, every Christian should be familiar with these truths which can set people free.

$5.95 + $1.50 Shipping/Handling

Impact Christian Books, Inc.
332 Leffingwell Avenue, Suite 101
Kirkwood, MO 63122

EXCITING NEW BOOK
ANSWERS AGE-OLD QUESTION

The author draws upon the Scriptural patterns and keys established by the Prophet Daniel to present readily understandable methods any believer can employ to *Tap into the Wisdom of God*. He shows from Scripture that it is both God's intention and will for man to turn to Him as the Source of knowledge.

You will learn seven major keys to receiving knowledge and find at least twenty-one practical encouragements to build your faith to seek God for answers.

Plus a Revelation

Discover for yourself the fascinating and prophetic secrets contained in Daniel Chapter Six, presented in the ninth chapter of this book. Chapter nine, which is actually a bonus book, presents an apparently undiscovered revelation showing more than one hundred parallels between Daniel and Jesus Christ.

"The most exciting thing I discovered was that what God did for Daniel, He can do for any believer!"

P.M., Bible Teacher, Kansas.

$10.95 + $1.50 Shipping

Impact Christian Books, Inc.
332 Leffingwell Ave., Suite 101,
Kirkwood, MO 63122

The
Acts
of
Pilate

ANCIENT RECORDS RECORDED BY
CONTEMPORARIES OF JESUS CHRIST
REGARDING THE FACTS CONCERNING
HIS BIRTH, DEATH, RESURRECTION

♦

TRANSLATED FROM THE ORIGINAL LANGUAGES
BY DRS. MCINTOSH and TWYMAN

♦

EDITED BY REV. W.D. MAHAN

This book was a favorite of the late Kathryn Kuhlman who often read from it on her radio show.

Early Church Writers such as Justin refer to the existence of these records, and Tertullian specifically mentions the report made by Pilate to the Emperor of Rome, Tiberius Caesar.

Chapters Include:
- *How These Records Were Discovered,*
- *A Short Sketch of the Talmuds,*
- *Constantine's Letter in Regard to Having Fifty Copies of the Scriptures Written and Bound,*
- *Jonathan's Interview with the Bethlehem Shepherds   Letter of Melker, Priest of the Synagogue at Bethlehem,*
- *Gamaliel's Interview with Joseph and Mary and Others Concerning Jesus,*
- *Report of Caiaphas to the Sanhedrim Concerning the Resurrection of Jesus,*
- *Valleus's Notes — "Acta Pilati," or Pilate's Report to Caesar of the Arrest, Trial, and Crucifixion of Jesus,*
- *Herod Antipater's Defense Before the Roman Senate in Regard to His Conduct At Bethlehem,*
- *Herod Antipas's Defense Before the Roman Senate in Regard to the Execution of John the Baptist,*
- *The Hillel Letters Regarding God's Providence to the Jews, by Hillel the Third*

THE ACTS OF PILATE $9.95, plus $2.00 Shipping

IMPACT CHRISTIAN BOOKS, INC.
332 Leffingwell Ave., Suite 101, Kirkwood, MO 63122

Impact Christian Books

332 Leffingwell Ave., Suite 101
Kirkwood, MO 63122